■ An antivivisectionist group placed a bomb in the yard of a Chicago researcher's home in early 1982. The bomb burned out before triggering an explosion that "would certainly have killed the family dog." The story did not identify the group or print the exact date of the attempted bombing. (*Chicago Tribune*, "Foes of Animal Research Baring Teeth in Protest," March 20, 1983.)

■ A letter bomb, sent to the office of former British Prime Minister Margaret Thatcher, scorched the face and hair of an office manager. Three similar incendiary letter bombs were sent on the same day to several members of the British Parliament, but were detected before they exploded. The Animal Rights Militia claimed responsibility. (November 30, 1982)

■ Researchers at the University of British Columbia were subjected to threatening telephone calls, hate mail and had antivivisectionist slogans spray-painted on their homes. One protester threatened to break the kneecaps of the university coordinator of the Animal Care Center. (1982)

■ Animal rights militants sent letter bombs to Britain's agricultural minister, Canada's diplomatic mission, the University of Bristol's Veterinary School in Weston-Super-Hare in Western England, and a scientist's home in Cambridge. (February 5, 1983)

■ Approximately 500 police officers were needed during an animal rights protest at a mink breeding farm near Warwickshire, England. Ironically, police horses were injured when the officers tried to contain the 2,000 demonstrators. Protesters released some of the mink, who escaped into the woods. Some were later found dead, presumably because they were unable to survive on their own. (January 29, 1984)

■ In England, the Animal Liberation Front turned to product tampering to publicize the use of animals used for testing. Bottles of shampoo that were contaminated with bleach were found in drug stores in London, Leeds and Southhampton after ALF issued a warning that the shampoo might be dangerous.

■ To protest the use of monkeys in tooth decay research, the Animal Liberation Front in England announced that its members had injected rat poison into selected Mars Bars chocolate candy already on store shelves. The manufacturer of the candy removed the candy bars from stores. (November 18, 1984)

■ The National Cancer Institute was notified that an Allentown, Pennsylvania, newspaper received a letter from the Animal Liberation Front stating that an institute would be bombed to protest Dr. Robert Weinberg's cancer research at the Whitehead Institute in Cambridge, Massachusetts. Dr. Weinberg also received threatening letters signed by ALF. The letters protested Weinberg's use of laboratory animals. A recent issue of *Science* reported that he uses tissue cultures, not live animals for experiments. (November 28, 1984)

■ Bomb threats were made against the University of Nevada School of Medicine as a protest against animal research. (November 30, 1984)

■ The Animal Liberation Front claimed responsibility for placing two gasoline bombs outside the London home of Nobel Laureate Sir John Vane, director of research and development at the Wellcome Foundation. The fire was extinguished before it spread beyond the garage. A second bomb was thrown at the residence of another Wellcome administrator and four employees had missiles launched through their windows and their properties covered with paint. (January 7, 1985)

■ Animal Liberation Front members left a threatening note and splattered red paint on the home and car of a Los Angeles County animal control officer as a protest against the sale of unclaimed pound animals to research laboratories. According to United Press International, the officer had received threatening calls from ALF. (March 11, 1985)

# THE HIJACKING

# of the

# HUMANE MOVEMENT

## by ROD & PATTI STRAND

Doral Publishing
Wilsonville, Oregon
1993

Published by Doral Publishing, PO Box 596, Wilsonville OR 97070.
Printed in the United States of America.
Cover design by Jill Regez
Cover art by Mary Jung


Library of Congress Number: 92-81328
ISBN: 0-944875-28-9


Strand, Rod
      Hijacking of the humane movement: animal
extremism/by Rod and Patti Strand. —
Wilsonville, OR : Doral Pub., © 1993.

      p. 174;cm.
      Includes bibliographical references
      ISBN: 0-944875-28-9


      1. Animal rights movement—United States.
      2. Animal rights activists—United States—
      Controversial works. I. Strand, Patti
      II. Title.
HV4764.8            179.3'0973  dc20
                        92-81328

# About the Authors

Rod and Patti Strand have enjoyed raising, breeding and showing Dalmatians under the Merry-Go-Round kennel name for more than 23 years in the Pacific Northwest. Their line of dogs is widely recognized for its exceptional quality and good temperament, as well as for the many champions and best-in-show winners it has produced. They've benefited tremendously from the human/animal bond and have watched as others have grown through positive associations with animals. They know that the human/animal bond is good for both people and animals, and that animals serve bona fide human needs in myriad ways. They believe that ending human relationships with animals, as animal rightists advocate, would have devastating consequences on human development and far-reaching effects on society.

The Strands have written extensively about the animal rights movement and its philosophy in an effort to clarify the differences between animal welfare and animal rights. Patti is executive director of the National Animal Interest Alliance, has appeared on radio and television, and has spoken to a wide range of audiences, from local to national levels, regarding the animal rights movement and its implications for society.

*The mad man shouted in the market place, no one stopped to answer him. Thus, it was confirmed that his thesis was incontrovertible.*
Dag Hammarshkjold, Secretary General of the United Nations

*It is important to answer the madman. It is important because, left unanswered, his lies and his malice can poison the climate. They can do worse. They can make other men mad. Left unanswered for long enough, they can nourish everything in men and women that is hateful and destructive and murderous. Our end is to ensure that every time the madman shouts in the market place, he is answered.*
Roy McMurtry, Attorney General of Ontario

# ACKNOWLEDGMENTS

In writing this book, we add our words to a small but growing chorus of others who have answered and continue to answer, sometimes despite considerable pressure to do otherwise. This list could be much longer, but so could the list of willing signatories to the *amicus curiae* brief submitted in support of Bobby Berosini in his defamation suit against PETA. For those who have worked to expose the true nature of animalism, but who have no desire to be named and targeted by animal rights extremists, THANK YOU for your assistance. We especially thank Bobby and Joan Berosini for being the first to swing back at the movement and for sharing their time and information. Special thanks to David Hardy, Esq., for the tremendous job he did in organizing and explaining the movement through his publications; and to Katie McCabe of *The Washingtonian*, whose outstanding articles gained her a whopping lawsuit. Thanks to Adrian Morrison, whose speaking out gained him intercontinental harassment and death threats. Thanks to Kathleen Marquardt and Mark LaRochelle of Putting People First for recognizing the seriousness of the issue early on and for donating their time and effort to increase public awareness of the problem. Thanks to Shirley Landa for gathering and sharing volumes of information and also to *Kennel Review* magazine for printing the truth when few others would risk putting it in print. We wish also to thank publisher Dr. Alvin Grossman, without whom this book simply wouldn't exist.

# TABLE OF CONTENTS

# FOREWORD

There comes a time when one must draw a line in the sand and say NO MORE!

The time has come for all those people who sincerely have the welfare of animals and society at large to declare to those misbegotten souls of the animal rights movement that we have had enough.

We laughed when they began their escapades and chortled when they dressed in those funny costumes. We coughed a bit when they began to throw blood on those wearing furs and became apprehensive when they tried to ram ships at sea. We became downright angry when they burst into research laboratories, freeing animals and destroying valuable research records. Our anger knew no bounds as they spray painted and firebombed their way into the public consciousness.

Then came the legislative campaigns to malign, hinder and demean breeders of purebred dogs and cats. This coupled with their attempted takeovers of Humane Societies and the well-planned mail campaigns to gather funds for their so-called legitimate activities.

In this book, Patti and Rod Strand help us look at what lies under the tip of the iceberg. As layer after layer is plumbed, we begin to feel the gorge rising as we realize we, the public, have been cleverly duped by mass media campaigns and the support of a few misguided stars of the entertainment world.

Read on and learn. The people are fighting back.

Dr. Alvin Grossman

# IN THE BEGINNING...

The humane movement has been hijacked, radicalized and rerouted. Started more than a hundred years ago, it was traditionally concerned with the humane treatment of animals. In the last 20 years, however, it has been taken over by animal rights leaders whose priority is neither the humane care of animals nor the prevention of cruelty to animals, but instead, the promotion of a revolutionary value system which redefines man's relationship with other animals. Animal rightists want to end man's use of animals altogether.

For those who are not directly involved with animals, the concept of danger from the humane movement's organized lunatic fringe may still seem remote, but to people who are daily involved with animals through professional, scientific, sporting, agricultural or other pursuits, the tactics used by these radicals to push their views and raise money are no longer dismissed lightly. These tactics include firebombing, burglary and attempted murder. They include the covert infiltration and takeover of organizations with differing views—redirecting their agendas and treasuries, corporate raider style, in the process.

Tactics also include prospecting for likely fundraising targets, such as institutions, individuals or newsworthy issues that can be exploited and sold to the public as representing cruelty to animals or damaging to the environment. Once the target is located, tactics can include systematic defamation or gross misrepresentation to create public outrage and thereby bring in the money. And bring in the money they do. Animal rights issues, especially those that concern gross examples of animal suffering and wanton abuse (known collectively in direct-mail circles as animal pornography), raise hundreds of millions of dollars annually.

To people who know the real mode of operation, the carnival atmosphere of the animal rights movement hides a true beast. While animal activists gain media attention with such antics as dressing up as bunnies and broccoli spears or by stripping down and bungee jumping nude, the victims of the animal rights movement recognize that a big part of its success occurs precisely because the beliefs and goals are beyond what a rational person is capable of believing: Themes, such as the PROMOTION OF SURGICAL EXPERIMENTATION ON BRAIN-DEAD HUMANS TO SAVE ANIMAL LIVES, ETHICAL VEGETARIANISM TO SAVE BOTH HUMAN SOULS AND THE PLANET FROM GLOBAL WARMING and the belief that PET OWNERSHIP IS THE MORAL EQUIVALENT OF SLAVERY, are all so radical that most people discount the whole movement as being too far out to take seriously or worry about.

Johnny Carson summed up American consciousness about the animal rights movement perfectly when he commented during his Tonight Show monologue that he had just four words to say about them: "Too much free time!" With such bizarre surface behavior being so amenable to one-liners and so subject to dismissal as prankster hijinks, it's no wonder that Americans aren't worried about the movement. Neither television anchors nor their viewing audiences have yet made any connection between firebombed university labs and the serious, fundamentalist philosophy of the parading, bungee-jumping vegetarians known as *animal rights*.

The animalists, by contrast, take themselves very seriously. They believe that the continuation of life itself on the planet earth is dependent on universal acceptance of the equality of all animals, and they are working around the clock to legislate this egalitarian relationship with animals into law. Their philosophy embraces a dream world that is sort of a new-age Eden in which the use of animals by humans is strictly taboo and humans commune with the rest of the natural world as equals. Somehow, the political, non-profit model used by the animal rights movement to effect this change has become one of the sneakiest and most powerful agents for social change in America. It changes public opinion through emotional, fundraising appeals which turn donors into activists. Through this supposedly educational process, everybody gets lobbied (enlightened) and the animal rights groups get rich while they promote laws that support their version of utopia.

Because they're not in it for the money—as evidenced by their non-profit status—our culture has naively bought into the proposition that they represent no special interest: hence, our cultural norms have allowed them to speak for the public at large, and against special for-profit interests. It is just now becoming obvious that non-profit as used by animal-rightist and environmental-extremist interests defines a very special world view indeed, and one at odds with the basic culture under whose institutions they are allowed to thrive. One that is working to see those institutions replaced.

Laws framed for public consumption as protections for lab animals, marine mammals and for the environment have been passed by the hundreds over the last two decades, and additional hundreds of animal-rights ordinances and bills are being pushed throughout the country. The numbers grow geometrically. Trapping, hunting, fishing, predator control, endangered species and biomedical research have been targets for years and continue to endure ever greater pressures. Dog and cat breeding, simply owning a pet, and certain segments of the food production and entertainment industries are being smeared in the public eye and legislated out of existence. All are taking on a new and impossibly complicated look. Every activity involving animals is getting more expensive, politically incorrect, complex and/or dangerous for institutions and individuals. And this is all possible because legislation and attitude changes are occurring alongside our natural concerns for sensible stewardship of the planet and the humane care of its inhabitants—under our noses, too close up for clear focus.

This movement has a layered structure that makes identification and definition almost impossible. It operates with incremental successes on many apparently innocuous, unrelated and/or unpopular fronts. These discrete actions are orchestrated carefully in each case to look like the morally right thing to do. However, these actions clearly work together to produce an ultimately destructive and morally repugnant result. The animal rights movement basically attacks people on moral grounds, one group at a time, shaming, and dividing and conquering as they go. Each group is played off against the others as being the repulsive one. Remember fur? Now it's pets! Awhile back it was *butchering* researchers. It's an effective mode of operation because in the West, man/animal interactions, unless considered abusive by law, have always been governed by personal value judgments within the context of an individual's religious freedom and democratic values. People simply are not prepared to defend their morals to another person—especially strangers whose morals they know nothing about. The resulting battle, which if scandalous enough is reported by the media, is truly bizarre. In the media battle that ensues, the animalists often are portrayed most favorably since they alone had pre-rehearsed the part.

Animal rights is a top-down, non-democratic kind of movement. It is served by many levels and obscured to the public by many layers of activism. The above-ground groups, (which may include the nude bungee jumpers), often serve as apologists for the criminal actions of the Animal Liberation Front. They are not classified as terrorist organizations themselves, but have been known to pump up their followers with such inflammatory, hateful and focused rhetoric that murder has been attempted for the cause. Leader-activists in the United States have been estimated at only 300 while the movement claims 10 million American followers. According to surveys, the rank and file membership often have no concept of the extreme positions promoted by the leadership. Many of these followers, when interviewed, actually hold moderate, animal welfare beliefs, but through contributing to animal rights organizations they have unwittingly become paid-up supporters of whatever extremism the leadership undertakes.

The Animal Liberation Front, or ALF as they spray-paint their calling card, is the international terrorist arm of the animal rights movement. ALF has used death threats, harassment, firebombing, explosives, crowbars and acid on such a broad scale that in England, Scotland Yard created a special division to deal with animal rights terrorism and in the U S, the FBI tracks them as a domestic terrorist group.

It is important to recognize the animal rights moment for what it is. Once a person sees behind the rhetoric and publicity stunts and begins to recognize the high-tech fundraising capabilities, the 10 million American disciples and the relentless wave of criminal acts claimed by the ALF, the more clear it becomes that releasing animals from *human bondage* is a deadly serious goal rather than an idle pastime of a bunch of fun-loving vegetarians with too much free time. In fact, the animal anarchists of this movement demonstrate a clear-cut way of operating that is at odds with our democratic institutions and way of life. The animal rights movement secret of success has been its ability to operate in the dark while posing as just another minority interest that deserves all the protections of our evolving liberal traditions. This operation appears to serve animals only when it is tactically in the rightists' immediate best interests. They maintain no shelters, preferring instead to obtain real estate where animal rights leaders may live in lovely settings called animal sanctuaries that offer limited programs for animals. Their most consistent characteristic is not the protection of animals; but rather, through the use of misinformation, public humiliation, intimidation and terrorism, the practice of animal rights hurts people.

Hundreds of criminal actions and millions of dollars in property damage have been claimed by ALF. But monetary tallies of the destruction, however many millions are involved, don't even hint at the depth of the tragedy that a firebombed laboratory signifies. Money cannot replace the loss of a human life. Nor can monetary assessments describe the psychological toll inflicted upon biomedical researchers and their families by death threats, character assassinations and the violent destruction of a lifetime's work. How do these values relate to the lives of lab animals, 90 percent of whom are laboratory-bred rodents? What does this say about the value of human life in our times? The activist's answer is clear.

In order to explain how we've arrived at this point in history, an overview of human/animal relationships will open our inquiry. Following that, we'll look at the development of the humane movement in England and 19th Century America, the exploitation of the animal symbol in Nazi Germany and the structure and goals of the movement as it exists today in England and the United States.

We'll look at some casualties of the movement, the stories of people whose lives have been altered and damaged by the actions of the animal rights extremists. And finally, we'll offer some suggestions and resources for use in contending with animal rights extremism and some parting observations on the origins and growth of this movement—the growth of cynicism and the resultant devaluation of human life.

dark while posing as just another minority interest that deserves all the protections of our evolving liberal traditions. This operation appears to serve animals only when it is tactically in the rightists' immediate best interests. They maintain no shelters, preferring instead to obtain real estate where animal rights leaders may live in lovely settings called animal sanctuaries that offer limited programs for animals. Their most consistent characteristic is not the protection of animals; but rather, the use of misinformation, public humiliation, intimidation and terrorism, and the practice of animal rights to hurt people.

Hundreds of criminal actions and millions of dollars in property damage have been claimed by ALF. But monetary tallies of the destruction, however many millions are involved, don't even hint at the depth of the tragedy that a firebombed laboratory signifies. Money cannot replace the loss of a human life. Nor can monetary assessments describe the psychological toll inflicted upon biomedical researchers and their families by death threats, character assassinations and the violent destruction of a lifetime's work. How do these values relate to the lives of lab animals, 90 percent of whom are laboratory-bred rodents? What does this say about the value of human life in our times? The activist's answer is clear.

In order to explain how we've arrived at this point in history, an overview of human/animal relationships will open our inquiry. Following that, we'll look at the development of the humane movement in England and 19th Century America, the exploitation of the animal symbol in Nazi Germany and the structure and goals of the movement as it exists today in England and the United States.

We'll look at some casualties of the movement, the stories of people whose lives have been altered and damaged by the actions of the animal rights extremists. And finally, we'll offer some suggestions and resources for use in contending with animal rights extremism and some parting observations on the origins and growth of this movement—the growth of cynicism and the resultant devaluation of human life.

# SECTION I

## A History of the Animal Rights Movement

# CHAPTER 1. Man, Woman and Animal

*Animal liberationists do not separate out the human animal, so there is no rational basis for saying that a human being has special rights. A rat is a pig is a dog is a boy. They're all mammals.*

Ingrid Newkirk, National Director and co-founder,
People for the Ethical Treatment of Animals

*Not a single sparrow falls to the ground without your Father's knowledge...Fear not, ye are of more value than many sparrows.*

Jesus, New Testament, Matthew 10:29

The domestication of plants and animals that began at the end of the ice age marked a crucial turning point in human history. From that point on, the role of humans in the natural world was transformed. For more than a million years before the domestication of animals, humans had led a relatively stable existence as hunters and gatherers. In that role, they were just another species competing to eke out a living from the natural world of plants and other animals. But after domestication, humans dominated—rather than competed with—the rest of the world. Through their unique powers of reason (according to modern interpretations), humans ended their egalitarian relationship with the natural world and ascended to the head of the pack.

The advantages of domestication for humans were so great that from its ice age beginnings until the time of Christ (a period of about 10,000 years) more than half of the world's population converted to an agrarian lifestyle. Today, nearly 100 percent of the human race benefits from some form of agriculture while hunting and gathering societies have become so rare that *National Geographic* magazine covers them like endangered species in remote outposts of the world where they still exist. It's interesting to note that although agricultural practices, from the modern perspective, may seem like the most natural state of affairs possible for humanity, the time during which this relationship has existed represents an extremely small fraction of human history. That is, humans have spent 99 percent of their time on earth behaving as part of the natural order by hunting and gathering, and only 1 percent acting superior to the natural world by domesticating and controlling it.

Once this shift began, and as the natural world fell more and more under human domination, progressively better methods of agricultural food production evolved. The rate of these advances occurred slowly at first, but, along with other technological and industrial developments, with increasing momentum until finally reaching critical mass about 100 years ago. At that time, the rate of agricultural change virtually exploded compared to its pace of evolution during the preceding 12,000 years. Using an example close to home, in 1880, one in two Americans lived on a farm; today, the ratio is less than one in 50. Agricultural needs for the mass of society are now met by only a tiny fraction of the population: 2 percent in the U.S., leaving 98 percent of the population out of the process.

This shift progressively limited opportunities for people to share in the more naturally evolving relationships with animals that previous generations experienced. Today, despite nearly universal dependence on animals, people lack hands-on experience with them. The consequences of such an arrangement are understandable. Knowing little about animals, and without personally participating in their care, people are anxious about their relationships with them. Their separation from the rest of the animal world creates a vacuum of animal-related knowledge and leaves people with a powerful and unfulfilled urge to re-establish their historic connection with the earth and animals and to give meaning to that relationship.

Attempts to come to terms with this void can be recognized in the ever expanding growth of pet ownership and in the development of the humane movement in the last century, first in England and then in America. England, which has been called a nation of pet keepers shows a relationship between its pet-keeping habits, which have grown steadily over the last couple centuries, and its pattern of urbanization; one which the US seems to mimic, although always trailing by a few decades. Today, England is 90 percent urbanized, up from 20 percent in 1800. In the US, where about 70 percent of all families are now urban, pet keeping is practiced by more than half of all American families—the same number as lived on farms in 1880! It is obvious that the people who migrated to the cities didn't leave the farm completely behind. Other efforts to ease, heal, explain or control our relationship with animals come from less tangible sources.

The responsive chord struck by Disney's cartoon fantasies (which project human traits onto animals) probably reflects this need. Disney's first animated cartoon was released amidst America's mass exodus from the farm in 1928, and at just the time when the majority of Americans no longer had personal contact with animals. Economic collapse, international unrest and rapidly changing values at home provided further context. Disney's films have been criticized for their anthropomorphized and overly sentimental portrayals of animals, but however fantastic these portrayals were, they offered people a connection with the natural world through animals that they had only recently lost and were beginning to miss.

Myths with their symbolic animal representatives (bald eagles, spotted owls, and others) serve as reconnecting agents too, and in a very real sense act as modern-day spirit guides in debates such as the one that rages currently in the Pacific Northwest over old-growth-timber harvesting versus jobs. In this debate and many others, the animal symbol, through its mythic personality and face, encourages humans to identify with the devastation of natural resources through a species that would otherwise remain academic and distant. Similarly, oily, helpless birds and other images of damaged wildlife, whether pictured in an Alaskan oil spill or on a war-ravaged Middle East beach, reconnect people to the natural world and warn of its possible annihilation. While ancient creeds evolve and new religions emerge, the animal symbol is used everywhere, offering various interpretations and suggestions to ease human discomfort over our current relations with the natural world. And no matter what a person's first religion might be in this day and age, environmentalism is almost assuredly the second.

It is important to note that as our distance from earth and animals increases, and as the void of knowledge and anxiety over the separation increases, so our psychological need to address these imbalances becomes more pressing. And, just as less developed stages of medicine insured the success of snake oil sales (and snake oil salesmen), our current need for a meaningful earth/animal connection provides an opening for the promotion of extremist interpretations, solutions and exploitations.

Fantasy, myth and religion represent intuitive and imaginative ways of dealing with questions and solving problems. They provide the theories that drive scientific inquiry in the natural progression that leads eventually toward a knowledge-based, rational understanding of the world. As knowledge is accumulated, these myths and religions are transformed, and if they survive at all, may serve as interpreters of the new data—but they are not final answers. They are important elements in the search for knowledge and understanding but serve as stations en route to rational thinking rather than the final destination.

Unfortunately, it is in the extremists' nature to view their religion or world view as the final, complete answer. The acrimonious debates between the animal and environmental extremists and mainstream society rage because enforcement of their world view cannot exist unless the search for more information is stopped and existing rights are either suspended or reallocated. Such is the nature of animal rights fundamentalism whose goals are pursued with religious zeal precisely because their agendas arise from a different religion from the western ethic under whose institutions they are currently forced to operate.

The shrillness of the current debate over the treatment of animals obscures the fact that human concern for animals has represented the typical human/animal relationship throughout history. Today, the debate is framed as though there are two, black and white, philosophically opposing factions within mainstream society; one against animal mistreatment, and one in favor of it. In casting the issue of animal treatment this way, abuse or neglect, when they occur, represent sins rather than social problems reflecting ignorance, mental illness, alcoholism or some other human failing or tragedy. It thereby moves the issue out of the category of social problems for which rational solutions might be sought and found, and into the realm of a fundamentalist religion, which urges emotionally triggered responses based on easily manipulated intuitive premises rather than scientific ones. As Michael Fox, animal rights leader and vice president of the

Humane Society of the United States puts it: "It is human nature that is the problem, and the suffering of the animal kingdom and the destruction of the natural world under our inhumane dominion are symptomatic consequences."

This modern, nihilistic view of man (pushed by popular culture, cults and others with a vested interest in causing humans to feel guilty about their humanity) sometimes leads people to conclude uncritically that humankind has never cared about anything but itself, its own needs, petty pleasures and destructive appetites. But this picture demonstrates only a limited view. While this view accurately reflects that *Homo Sapiens* are driven by self-interest, as are all species, it fails to acknowledge the part of human nature that experiences love, awe and reverence for the earth, for humans and other living beings and which through reason, compassion and conscience, strives beyond its own self interest to create an ethical relationship with all. That is, humans make moral judgments routinely that transcend their own immediate best self-interest. The denial of this elemental human quality (a denial which the animal rights movement promotes) not only debases and diminishes the value of human life, it doesn't square with the historical record.

Our ancestors' relationship with animals is well recorded on the walls of caves, in architectural friezes and wooden totems that show that humans have always seen their relationship with animals in terms of reverence as well as dependency. Hunting and gathering societies practiced religious rituals in their hunting exercises as do modern aborigines who, with no training at all in Western thought, view their right to use and dominate animals as an ethically justifiable role in the natural order of things, since animal use by other animals is the way of the world.

Despite a history of ongoing use by humans, from the earliest records forward, and despite the reverential view of animals held by humans, it is clear that people have never practiced anything close to a universal code of behavior toward animals. Even when wide-spread social acceptance of a particular religion prevails, individual interpretations of that doctrine still mark human/animal ethical relationships. "Where's the beef?" may reveal the modern American position on beef eating, but our preference for hamburgers and prime rib is not a universal one. The sacred cow of India bears testimony to a different standard and famines have been recorded in which people have actually chosen to eat one another rather than violate their religious taboo against eating a particular species. Many Asian diets include the meat of dogs, but Americans who keep them as pets are repulsed by the idea. So it goes. The religions, folklore and mythologies of a particular society determine which animals are revered, which ones are used to benefit man (and how) and which ones are left alone. Strictly speaking, to the extent that religions reflect community values, the treatment of animals, both personally and by society, is religious in nature.

Major world religions offer guidelines for dealing with animals that include injunctions against certain practices and urgings to treat animals or view them in a specific way consistent with the larger doctrine. Since biblical times, the dominant belief system in the West has been based on the Judeo-Christian premise of human dominion and stewardship found in the Old Testament. In this tradition, dominion places humans in the position of *standing in* for God on earth as loving stewards or caretakers, with direct responsibilities to God and indirect responsibilities to animals for their welfare. That is, as we accept the right to use animals and other natural resources for our benefit, we must be responsible stewards who view the creation as good and therefore use its resources with reverence. All human life is considered sacred in this tradition.

Vegetarians sometimes use the creation story as a testimonial to God's true ideal for mankind since in *Genesis*, God lays a vegetarian table for man and wild animals alike, but the story of the ark and the historical world after the flood in which man is forced to live, points to another conclusion: in this setting, where life comes from death, wild animals are predator and prey and innocent children suffer terrible diseases, humans are given animals to eat. Since Abel kept sheep even before the flood, and since the biblical concept of responsible care includes provisions for their humane slaughter, meat eating like most other animal usage is actually a background fact rather than a point of biblical debate. Likewise, the use of furs is a given, since God put animal skins on Adam and Eve before they even left the Garden. Regarding hunting, Hebrew writings indicate that hunting animals for meat is a proper role, whereas shooting an animal for sport and leaving it to rot is not. The latter would come under the designation of wanton cruelty since it represents a capricious, senseless killing that offers no benefit. Summing up, the Judeo-Christian tradition simply recognizes that humans use animals and asks that we do so with reverence for all creation.

By contrast, Eastern religions (only known in the West for the last two centuries) stress the interconnectedness of all life forms and promote a value system that de-emphasizes the importance of man in the overall scheme of things. They elevate, as an overriding value, the web of life, a value that is exalted in the modern environmental and new-age movements as well. Against this new context, the Judeo-Christian tradition is seen as being too anthropocentric, not sufficiently biocentric and therefore ecologically unbalanced. Animalists find Eastern doctrines more aligned with their beliefs than Western.

It's the fundamental premise of the animal rights philosophy that when humans domesticated animals they altered the human relationship with the natural world to one that assures the ecological destruction of the planet. The animal rights revulsion to the Judeo-Christian premise of human dominion and stewardship found in the Old Testament is therefore predictable, since quite literally, domestication equals dominion. Rightists believe that by using their rational faculties to domesticate animals, humans tilted the playing field unfairly to one which enslaved the rest of creation.

They, along with many other new-world order groups, think that dominion translates to ruination and that it has been used in the Western ethical tradition as justification for raping and pillaging the earth and its inhabitants. Along with animalists, these new agers are represented by others, often called the new left, who have not found a home in traditional social structures: deep ecologists, post-conservation environmentalists, ethical and ecological vegetarians, radical feminists, and collectively, the anti-science contingency. They equate dominion to white male dominance and a worldview that is hierarchical, rather than egalitarian, capitalistic rather than socialistic and reductionistic, mechanistic and rational as opposed to spiritual, intuitive, holistic and ecological.

The Jewish and Christian faithful naturally defend the concept of dominion against the animalist position, saying it was not intended to give humans license to destroy the earth. They argue that interpreting dominion in a way that justifies suffering, waste and the destruction of animals and the rest of the natural world is a misrepresentation or perversion of scripture. What these apologists may not realize is that it does not matter to animalists how well animals are treated under human dominion: it is the fact that humans were arrogant enough to domesticate them in the first place that produces contempt. Animalists view other animals as innocently pursuing their self-interest when they survive at the expense of other animals. However, they conclude that because humans are self-aware and rational in pursuit of similar self-interests, their pursuits are tainted.

Because of the clear-cut chasm that lies between the dogmas of animal rights and the Judeo-Christian traditions, it's conceivable that when animal rights leaders include biblical images such as references to the "lion laying down with the lamb," they are appropriating those images to subvert or exploit the values held by others rather than because they are interested in saving or modernizing the old creed. There is just no getting around it; in the Western system, humans and animals do *not* have equal rights. In the "Golden Rule," the term *others* is not exclusive, but it does mean humans first! And this belief is part of Western thought even among people who have never been inside a church.

To explain where humans and animals fit relative to the natural world and to God in this belief system, Jesus advises in *Matthew*, in the first book of the New Testament, that not even one sparrow is forgotten by God, while comforting and advising man that he is of greater value than many sparrows. Here, reverence for all creation is affirmed, and the relative value symbolically implied between man and sparrow encourages humans to believe that if they don't hold special reverence for themselves, reverence for the rest of creation is impossible. To restate this concept in modern terms: "you can't love anyone or anything more than you love yourself." Reverence must start at home. It is specifically this Christian belief, that humans are special, that is unacceptable to animalists.

A comparison of the Christian belief with the position stated by animal rights leader, Ingrid Newkirk, underscores this interpretation: "Animal liberationists do not separate out the human animal, so there is no rational basis for saying that a human being has special rights. A rat is a pig is a dog is a boy. They're all mammals." Newkirk's explanation reveals that the animal-rights belief system emerges from an altogether different view of man: It neither holds human life in high esteem nor does it view human potential to grow, learn and improve with the same optimistic affection as does the Judeo-Christian tradition. Instead, just as other nihilistic, doctrinaire political movements have arisen this century to harmonize with and to exploit disillusionment, animalism reflects a pessimistic view of man. Nearly a hundred years ago, Frederick Nietzsche observed this growing contempt for humanity when he reflected: "What is modern day nihilism if it is not that, 'we are tired of man,'" thereby hinting at a looming tragedy, decades before the holocaust.

Pierre Proudhon, the 19th Century French revolutionary, asserted that "all controversies about public policy, if pursued far enough, turn out to be religious in nature. Disputants are separated by more than their immediate differences. Their argument is about premises, and premises come from systems of belief that are explicitly religious or, at least function like religions by providing a comprehensive way of viewing the world." Keeping this equation in mind, it would seem inevitable that if animal rightists and biocentric environmentalists have problems with the Judeo-Christian religious tradition, they would also have fundamental problems with Western democratic traditions. And they do.

Peter Singer, as one of the founders of the modern animal rights movement and author of *Democracy and Disobedience,* makes no pretense of support for Western religious traditions, stating matter-of-factly that Eastern traditions are superior as they relate to animals. Of course, Western democratic traditions fully support Singer's right to believe as he chooses: but significantly, animal rightists demonstrate they have no desire to return the favor. Their actions make it clear that they neither share Western religious traditions nor do they appreciate the Western democratic principles that arose from them, except when needed to protect their own rights.

While democracy affirms the value of humanity by stressing individual freedom, the evolving anti-democratic, anarchist, Nazi format of the animalists' developing political mode, emerges from a pessimistic view of human nature which devalues human life. Accordingly, like other nihilistic, dogmatic political movements this century, it works to limit individual freedom and favors control using regulation, coercion, propaganda and physical force as enforcement tools. Specifically, animalists have engaged in defamation of character, public humiliation, attacks on free speech, economic sabotage (which is one of the primary methods recommended by movement leaders), death threats, and the use of terrorism.

Fundamentalism is on the rise here and around the world. It's a danger everywhere it exists, but it represents a particularly pernicious threat on the inside of a representative system. Today, major parties exploit the tribal tendency for political interests to see their own worldview as superior to the system (even when their ascendancy would mean another group would thereby be deprived of basic democratic rights). They treat small minority interests, if the constituency is fanatical enough to vote as a monolithic bloc, as though they have a realistic chance to control public policy despite their minority status. The major parties thereby engage in the demise of their own government by abetting minority control. Both political parties have factions which systematically work to subvert majority views and enforce their will on society. The religious right pushes public policy decisions by purporting to speak for voiceless unborn babies with the support of people who not only block entrances to abortion clinics but sometimes bomb them; on the left, zealots purport to speak for voiceless trees, spotted owls and lab animals with a supporting fringe element who spike trees and destroy laboratories and mink farms. Both ends of the spectrum work to get legislation passed that the majority does not want. Both work relentlessly to subvert the democratic process to get their own version of utopia enacted. And in all cases, these extremists justify their actions by calling on a higher law. It's a part of their fundamentalist crusade to impose their ethics on us by whatever means it takes.

As an example of what this means, the Humane Society of the United States distributes a children's newspaper to public schools that appears to promote mainstream animal protectionism and wholesome environmentalism. However, the teacher's guide (which parents may never see) contains suggested exercises that clearly promote animalism, which is anti-human dominion. By contrast, if Baptists, Catholics, Jews or Scientologists put so-called educational materials in public schools that subversively promoted their worldviews, the public would be outraged. In fact, this is happening all across America, but the religion is animal rights rather than a doctrine we recognize.

Today, new creeds abound that collectively promote replenishing the earth through deindustrialization and throwing out science. The most dogmatic of these, and the only one with a terrorist arm, is the modern animal rights movement. Of all the new left groups, the animal rights movement offers us the best close-up glimpse of how new radical strategies are operating in Western democracies. Unlike the open opposition of the communist party, the KKK or even the skinheads and Nazis, through the tool of political correctness, the new left pretends to be part of and even to be motivated by the values of the democratic system as it systematically attempts to dismantle it.

The basic, ancient premise with which the animalists disagree, the domestication of animals, turns out to have far-reaching implications in our inquiry into the nature of animalist goals. Since domestication equals dominion, and dominion is a fundamental tenet of the Judeo-Christian belief system, the disagreement conveniently turns out to be an anarchist's ticket to justify, in the name of minority rights, relentless attacks on the Western ethic and on every business associated with animals in any way. This would include everything from livestock production to pharmaceuticals, clothing, animal research, entertainment, sports, transportation, and one's personal behavior with pets. And, when endangered species are added to the list through the new even more politically correct label of biodiversity, all human relationships with the natural world will be affected. Being anti-dominion is literally an anarchist's excuse to bash individual rights and liberties. Through the art form of political correctness, anarchists of all persuasions are learning the truth of another of Nietzsche saying: "Morality is the best of all devices for leading mankind by the nose."

It's difficult to imagine what a dominionless new age free of speciesism (the animal rightists' dominion-based term for racism between species) might be. Paul Watson, pioneer Greenpeace member and founder of the Sea Shepherd Conservation Society, offers a clue: "Under ecological law, a species' survival takes precedence over the individual rights of any other species." In 1987, when an Oregon logger took a saw blade in the face from a tree that had been spiked by an environmentalist extremist, Earth

First! pioneer Dave Foreman said that he was sorry, but: "I quite honestly am more concerned about old growth forests, spotted owls and wolverines and salmon—and nobody is forcing people to cut those trees."

Many rightists have clarified for us how they view their mission by stating: "We're in a war." George Cave, past president of Trans-Species Unlimited, gave anarchist clarification to that intent by advising: "The liberation of animal life can only be achieved through the overthrow of the existing power structure. Such a transition will be brought about only through a populist uprising of gigantic proportions." Cave apparently believes that after the uprising we can finally start peacefully coexisting with other living beings.

Since the animal rights movement systematically uses misinformation, disinformation, sensationalism, outright lies, public humiliation, defamation of character and "SLAPP" suits (Strategic Lawsuits Against Public Participation) to shut opponents' mouths, and fire bombings and death threats when those tactics don't work, we need to realize that they are serious and start taking them at their word.

In modern times the absence of natural experiences and relationships with animals causes human discomfort and drives people to seek new meanings and new relationships. Existing religions cover our relationship with animals, but no teachings within them cover our modern lack of relationship with them. There are none to explain their absence from our world. Many attempts have emerged in the last few centuries to fill this void and to heal this lost relationship. They are led today by a full spectrum of philosophers, reformers, ecologists, naturalists, charismatics, myth makers, anarchists and charlatans who try to respond, but in some cases, exploit instead, the emotional needs of urbanized society. These modern-day redeemers are, in fact, stepchildren of the humane movement founded more than a century ago in England, which was born to prescribe a new ethical human-animal relationship for urbanized society. ⊕

# CHAPTER 2. England: Where It All Began

*Medical science has arrived probably at its extreme limits. Nothing can be gained by repetition of experiments on living animals.*

Sir George Duckett, circa 1875

*English scientists should never have lowered the flag and let a parcel of sophists try to teach them morality and humanity; professors should have resigned rather than allow police regulation of research...In France, it was different. The Catholic religion gave old maids a necessary refuge, providing full satisfaction for 'the mystical and superstitious tendencies indigenous to the soil of the human mind.'*

Researcher Elle de Cyon, in a scornful attack on England's "pseudo-humanitarian movement" in 1883

The humane movement as we know it today began last century in England with the founding of the Society for the Prevention of Cruelty to Animals in 1824 (after 1840 it became the Royal SPCA) and the National Anti-Vivisection Society. Its emergence as a credible social movement marked both a starting point and a coming together of forces that had been gathering momentum for centuries. Set against a background of extraordinary cruelty to animals in Elizabethan and Victorian England, the Enlightenment, the growth of humanitarianism, Methodism and Darwinism lit the stage for a new look at human and animal relationships.

Through the Enlightenment, the *rights of man* became the topic of the age in Europe and the American Colonies, and public outrage over slavery soon raised consciousness about other areas of human suffering and misery as well. Women's suffrage, the treatment of animals, prisoners, and finally the treatment of the mentally ill became important subjects of debate and targets for reform.

Humanitarianism arose from every educational level, social class and religious denomination, although vegetarian John Wesley's Methodists led the crusade. The basic message, no matter who delivered it or what the intellectual trappings were, was simple: *kindness was better than cruelty.* Political philosophers promoted the idea that animals had a right not to be cruelly abused; Methodists gave sermons that encouraged people to think in terms of an expanded kingdom in which animals were included and people were invited to behave as angels, and to view animals as humans were now. Later, when Anglicans began to preach the same message, they were accused of being either insane or Methodists. Utilitarian philosophers such as Jeremy Bentham urged people not to discount the worth of animals because they could not reason as humans do, but instead to grant them kindness in consideration and recognition of their ability to suffer.

Moralists also worked for the cause, propagandizing that cruelty to animals leads to cruelty to people. They claimed that being abusive toward animals had the effect of demoralizing and hardening the heart of the perpetrator. Pamphleteers and artists joined hands with poets, playwrights and essayists in advocating benevolence to animals as a natural extension of human compassion. Finally, Darwin's theory of evolution demoted humans from their position of special relationship with God and put them into a biological "chain of being" with the rest of creation. These reassessments of man's ethical and biological relationship with animals caused Englishmen to take a fresh look at the brutality heaped on animals all around them; once refocused, they couldn't help noticing there was quite a lot to see.

In the Elizabethan Age, cruelty toward animals in England was perfected to the level of a national pastime—its popularity akin to baseball in the United States today. Indeed, the literature from the period suggests that the British worked feverishly to come up with ever more inventive and bizarre ways of tormenting, torturing and mutilating animals. Animals were pitted against one another in all sorts of gruesome blood sports to provide opportunities for amusement, sport and wagering. Bull- and bear-baiting contests were fashionable spectator sports for all classes, as were cock and dog fighting. Queen Elizabeth was a devotee of the *bear garden* herself, and when theater going started gaining popularity with the sporting crowd, Elizabeth ordered the theater closed on baiting night. In addition to being an avid sportswoman, the queen worried that play watching might put the new ideas about liberty into her subjects' minds.

During an animal baiting, the animal being baited was chained to a post while relays of dogs, often six at a time, were released to attack and taunt it amidst cheers of onlookers. Bears and bulls were the usual victims, but horses, dogs and other animals were baited as well. During a bear-baiting, the bear often maimed or killed a number of attacking dogs before the event was finally stopped by the bear warden. It was the warden's job to stop the event before the bear was killed so that he could live to fight another day. Those bears who survived repeated baitings were often recognizable from injuries they'd received in previous bouts; many were blinded by repeated eye lacerations. Paintings of baitings show grinning spectators having a whale of a good time.

Baiting was touted as having educational value as well as being entertainment. The common English perception was that witnessing baitings and other blood sports had the positive effect of turning observers into soldiers capable of defeating the French.

On a related note, the English took great pleasure in abusing the *cock* which just happened to serve as the French national emblem. In England, Shrove Tuesday, the last day of merriment before Lent, was actually set aside as a special day for "throwing at cocks." In this sport, the bird was tied to a stake and then, as the name implies, "thrown at" until it dropped over dead. Sometimes death came slowly and the cock had to be propped up with splints so that he could continue his demise by pummeling. Young children were encouraged to develop their skill in throwing and it's been recorded that even gentle Sir Thomas Moore was a talented, well-practiced "cocker" in his youth.

At Eton, cruelty to animals was so common and extreme, observers claimed that abuse of animals was part of the curriculum. The boys at Eton were always chasing, whipping or dissecting something, and the dissection part was often an extracurricular activity. At Eton, curiosity killed the cat— repeatedly.

Live dissection was all the rage in 17th Century Europe. Checking things out by experiment was the new pastime justified by Rene Descartes, the mathematician philosopher, who stated that animals had neither soul nor feelings but were unthinking machines, like clocks. Open season was declared on all animals, and vivisection was justified for all curious participants. Scientists and physicians were only a fraction of the number who had inquiring minds back then. Everyone was cutting and looking and wanting to know more. Ladies from the finest families watched disembowelings and the *new* intellectual pursuits were reported to be "dismembering, poisoning, drowning, suffocating, gutting, burning, impaling, draining, starving and injecting." No particular attempt was made to coordinate efforts or resulting data, and there was little interest in developing a scientific body of knowledge. It was simply a time when people wanted to take a closer look.

Dissection occurred outside the realm of inquiry, too. *The Sporting Magazine* of 1794 reported a truly astonishing feat that involved a less-scientific form of dismembering: The article testified that two guineas had been paid a Yorkshire shepherd after he successfully devoured a live tom cat on Fair Day. Later in the day, according to the story, the shepherd reported that he "was neither sick nor sorry." Similar stories are common in this era.

In England, the fox hunt was a popular sport. Englishmen believed that it bonded gentlemen (as distinguished from commoners, who ostensibly were already well-bound) with their dogs and land. For young men, it served as a rite of passage, too. After the fox was bagged, blood was rubbed all over the face of the initiate, whose eyes gleamed with uncontrolled excitement. The fact that many of the early members of the SPCA were fox hunters may account for the lack of criticism this sport received in the early days, compared to similar issues. Members claimed that foxes would destroy agriculture if not controlled by hunting even though foxes were frequently brought in for the sport. John Stuart Mill, the famous political philosopher and promoter of liberalism, turned down an offer to serve as vice president of the SPCA because of its fox-hunting members' tendency to find problems with lower class diversions such as baiting while quietly preserving their own questionable practices. He viewed them as hypocrites.

Sometime between the reigns of Elizabeth and Victoria, horses graduated from being regarded primarily as draft animals to sporting animals. Horsemanship became the rage, presenting new opportunities to maim and torture animals creatively. Books of the period disclosed unusual training methods for putting a little zip into an uncooperative steed. One method called for tying a shrewd cat to a pole and leaving its head and feet exposed, thrusting it to the underside of the horse's "cods." An even more devious, if not more painful plan, instructed the trainer to suspend a hedgehog under the tail of a horse where the beast's hissing would cause the horse to step out. Still another recommendation called for wrapping a knotted cord around a horse's "stones" and giving it a yank to get him going or to put his brakes on. Many stallions had to be gelded as a result of these and similar practices.

Horses used as draft animals were run to death and ones too weak to run were often run anyway, until they dropped. Afterwards, their carcasses were bid over in the streets by merchant vultures who arrived just as ambulance chasers show up at wrecks today. Sometimes the assessment of worth for a decrepit horse was calculated by figuring its value in terms of the number of working days it had left (during which it would no longer be fed because of its relative uselessness), and subtracting from that value its current worth in estimated immediately renderable flesh.

Horsemanship presented subtle opportunities for cruelty, too. The bearing ring was a cruel device that had a fair hand in launching the modern humane movement, with a little help from Anna Sewell's classic book, *Black Beauty,* The bearing ring made its debut in England around the beginning of the 19th Century and was immediately adopted in the United States as well. It made a horse hold its head constantly in a showy, high-styled pose, which prevented normal action and caused gouging of the mouth. The result was that the horse was always unnaturally reined up and back, couldn't use his body efficiently going up or down hills and couldn't see where he was going. Often a reddish-tinged foam spewed from his mouth as a result of the gouging caused by the bit, which bore down under the tongue. The usage of the bit also became an issue of class since it was primarily the rich who persisted in its use and its advocacy. To mock the rich, cartoons depicted aristocrats with their heads thrust up and back, too, and tongues hanging from open mouths. A law outlawing it was not passed in England until 1911, but public opinion turned against it quickly as a result of Miss Sewell's book and the class issue, which is still an effective tool in humane issues such as fur today.

By 1822, the first bill opposing wanton animal cruelty, the Martin Act, passed into British law. Ironically, the first SPCA was formed because this law proved to be unenforceable. Through the SPCA, with officers made up of well-known humanitarians, including Richard Martin himself (known as "Humanity Dick"), numerous anti-cruelty laws were passed and enforced. Finally, the Act of 1835 outlawed the "bastard sport of baiting," which had been practiced for 700 years in England, but which by then was only popular among the poor. At the time baiting was finally outlawed, though, live-cat skinning was still commonplace on London streets and pig whipping (a pre-slaughter tenderizing process) was still practiced in the gourmet kitchens. The image of the SPCA was greatly enhanced when Victoria became its patron. When she ascended the throne and became queen, *Royal* was added to its name, making it the Royal Society for the Prevention of Cruelty to Animals—the oldest animal protection agency in the world.

To put animal cruelty and the growth of the English humane movement in a more understandable context, it must be recalled that until the dawn of the Elizabethan Age in England, 1547 to be exact, people were still being lobbed into boiling oil as punishment for various crimes. Mentally ill patients provided Saturday night entertainment for a public who regarded bedlam as a sort of amusement park or spectacle for their viewing pleasure until reforms centuries later. And at the beginning of the 19th Century, 200 capital offenses still remained on the English statute books.

The idea that animals deserved protection from wanton cruelty was championed by Mill, Bentham, Martin, Lawrence and later Thoreau, Salt (an ex-schoolmaster at Eton) and others. Beyond them, there weren't many social thinkers of that period who were sufficiently educated to stay abreast of the evolution of rights theories. For most Englishmen, the subtleties and sophistication of liberalism as it applied to animals were lost. Far more important for the masses in developing an humane ethic were common sense and popular culture, including plays and poems, sentimentality and religious beliefs. At the same time, and in an urbanizing climate that parallels the period a half century later in the United States when the humane movement took off here, fewer people were involved with animal agriculture than had been at any time previously, and the fear of wild beasts was diminishing. Just as importantly, more people were bringing pets into their homes where they demonstrated love, intelligence, loyalty and that they could, in fact, feel pain. Even so, the most progressive animal advocates of the period held animal welfare positions and no one really challenged the idea that humans had the right to use animals for food, clothing and as draft animals, so long as they were treated humanely. The reformers who founded the humane movement simply wanted the animals under human dominion to be treated with compassion.

Not all were inspired by pure compassion for animals, however. Many educated Victorians were obsessed with theology and believed that science and spirituality were at fundamental odds. They, like the group that called themselves the Luddites earlier in the century, feared science. The Victorians sided with their own religious interpretations against science and technology, while the Luddites sided with manual labor over a technology they believed would render them obsolete. Victorian activists, like the antivivisectionists, Francis Power Cobbe, Sir Duckett and many others, vocalized a related, but slightly different sentiment: People deserved the diseases they possessed and therefore did not deserve to be cured, especially through the use of animal research which harmed innocent animals. They also argued that there was nothing more to learn and that additional research represented unnecessary duplication.

Some were sentimentalists concerned more with their own reactions to animal suffering than to the animals themselves. Miss Cobbe has been accused of this and the related practice of anthropomorphism, projecting human traits onto animals and then judging them by human standards. Distinctions between hurting and killing are not made by the sentimentalist while anthropomorphic projections lead people to buy dog food designed to appeal to human palates rather than the digestive tracts of dogs. Humane concern, on the other hand, considers the animal, not our human reaction to it. On this score, the 20th Century psychiatrist Karl Menninger observed that the antivivisection movement was a clear-cut example of reaction formation: people overreacting to their own impulses of cruelty by attempting to forbid activities on the part of others which they believe to be cruel. This, he claimed, actually increased the amount of suffering in the world.

Still other motives combine fuzzy thinking about animal protectionism with even less noble intentions—the desire to punish others. Along with genuinely compassionate and humane participants, the humane movement has always had a large supply of these sentimentalists and punishers, people who do not fit in, are fearful of science and are looking for someone to blame for their feelings of pain. Today, with the help of a terrorist wing, fundraising know-how and media sophistication, the modern animal rights movement is able to recruit and exploit these feelings of frustration selectively. More alarmingly, the modern animal rights movement uses the so-called love for animals as a conversion device for teaching hatred of humans, including self-hatred. "Because of humans, pet slaughter goes on!" reads one Seattle-area headline for an article prompted by Mitchell Fox of the radical Progressive Animal Welfare Society. Although countless examples such as this one exist, no clearer expression of using a scapegoat is needed to show that blaming people is part of the program or belief system that drives the animal rights concern for animals.

A couple of decades after the founding of the RSPCA in England, the United States humane movement was launched in earnest. The first was the American Society for the Prevention of Cruelty to Animals, founded in 1866, by New Yorker Henry Bergh and modeled carefully after the British RSPCA prototype. Bergh was inspired by the leaders of the RSPCA during a stopover in London. The degree of Bergh's inspiration is reflected in his declaration of rights for animals in the charter of the ASPCA. He emphasized protections for domesticated animals primarily, but that emphasis served as a springboard for promotion of revolutionary legislation that forbade cruelty to all animals, even "unowned" animals previously outside the scope of the law.

Cut from the same cloth as their British sponsors, American humane leaders had begun their political careers as abolitionists, child-welfare reformers and women's rights advocates whose humanitarian convictions ran deep. Horses were everywhere and abuses were easy to spot. In England, Anna Sewell's book, *Black Beauty: His Groom and Companions,* outraged readers against the use of the bearing ring and cruelty to horses. George T. Angell, founder of the Massachusetts Society for the Prevention of Cruelty of Animals, was also a horse lover and despised the bearing ring. Angell believed Anna Sewell's *Black Beauty* could serve the horse in the way that Harriet Beecher Stowe's book, *Uncle Tom's Cabin,* had served the abolition of slavery. He made it his personal mission to print and put *Black Beauty* into mass circulation. Anna Sewell died the year following her book's publication without knowing its impact. More than a century later, children still read it and in doing so develop their compassion for animals. Due to its overwhelming effect, Anna Sewell is remembered today as a great humanitarian.

Angell founded his SPCA as a response to witnessing a horse race in which the first- and second-place winners died. Through his organization, he distributed thousands of pamphlets speaking against cruelty to horses and the use of the bearing ring, and he posted signs commanding horsemen to slacken their reins. He is also credited with disseminating the first humane periodical, *Our Dumb Animals*, and with founding the American Humane Educational Society, as well as an American version of the RSPCA's children's group, the Bands of Mercy. (He would roll over in his grave if he learned about the modern version of the Bands of Mercy, which will be discussed in a later chapter.) Angell, who liked people *and* animals, noticed the benefits of the human-animal bond. He realized, after surveying a prison, that the convict population consisted primarily of men who had never had pets as children. This spurred his resolve to bring animals and humans closer together for mutual benefit.

Drawings and articles from the American Colonies show that many of the blood sports of England were imported and in common practice. Horses were driven to death and surplus dogs were muzzled and shot to death in annual hydrophobia frenzies. Barbaric practices, which included frivolous infliction of pain and suffering on animals, were commonplace. One particularly graphic sketch shows an entertainer biting heads off rats for a fee (one is glad not knowing what this chap did for an encore).

Shooting sports were practiced everywhere. In America, these sports often, but not always, produced food. The American wilderness provided people with a tangible connection to a natural world no longer present in many European countries: a place where until recent decades man could recognize his part in the natural world and feel comfortable taking his place in it.

Other SPCAs followed and during the next quarter of a century, local humane societies became part of the mainstream American landscape. Antivivisection organizations, although never truly mainstream, started adding their numbers to the animal scene during this period, thereby defining the outer limits of the humane movement in 19th Century America.

Anesthetic relief from pain for animals at this time was no better than that available for humans; for whom the term *bite the bullet* held special significance. In short, pain and suffering were excruciating by today's standards in both human medicine and animal research. The drive by antivivisectionists during this time used the absence of anesthetic development as a lever to argue against all animal experimentation. The continued use of animals in research, however, led directly to anesthetic relief for humans and animals alike.

The efforts of the antivivisectionists climaxed in 1896 with the near passage of a bill to regulate animal research. It's failure is attributed to the fact that in this same time frame animal research was used to produce an antitoxin that dramatically reduced diphtheria deaths.

During the decades surrounding the American Civil War, prominent minds had begun debating the possibility that *natural rights* should be extended even beyond the human community. Most of the emphasis was aimed at eliminating willful cruelty to domestic animals, but some suggested more. Scientists, like Darwin, had pointed out man's similarity and relationship to other animals, and Darwin's personal notes reflected a conscious choice not to frame this relationship in such hierarchical terms as "higher" or "lower" animals. His scientific view of an entire biological system and his actions as a scientists, however, supported dominionist inquiry, including the practice of vivisection.

Religious leaders such as Henry Ward Beecher (Harriet Beecher Stowe's brother) urged that children respect all creatures, even insects and worms. Bergh, founder of the first American SPCA, suggested that animals might cohabit with humans in heaven. Thoreau's journals bore testimony to an evolving ecological ethic in which man "participated" with stars, fish, birds and trees in an extended community; and his work questioned human dominion. Harriet Beecher Stowe took her reputation as an abolitionist, social activist and reformer into the humane movement with a passion, comparing the caging of animals with slavery and paving the way for the *true believers* of the next century who would like to transfer human standards of ethical treatment to the "voiceless constituencies" of animals. This philosophy ushered in an age in which liberalism might also be allowed to speak for spotted owls, trees and rivers, an age in which extremists and fundraising junkies would speak for the ethical treatment of animals, an age in which the systematic destruction of the entire Western ethic in an era of human disillusionment would finally be politically correct.

By the end of the 19th Century, the humane movement had peaked and was starting to ebb in the United States. Accused of sentimentalism, some 20th Century animal radicals declared that the early humane movement actually slowed the progress for animals and the environment. They pointed out that, for the most part, humane workers and animal moralists of that period never got beyond Locke and Mill in viewing kindness to animals as valuable to human moral development. This view was held primarily because the *kindness* of the period had the notable dividend of a positive effect on the humans involved. Moreover, it was utilitarian or instrumental (or as current jargon would dub it, wise-use oriented), stressing the economic good sense it made to care for one's animal property properly.

By today's animal activist standards, the turn of the century humane movement was guilty of promoting the ethically and ecologically bankrupt ideas of dominion and stewardship, rather than recognizing the emerging egalitarian model (destined to be run by an ethically superior elite).

Notwithstanding this battering of a growing ideal, after its importation from England, the humane movement of the 19th Century spurred many advances for animals here. Thoreau and others of the 19th Century had set the foundation for the holistic environmentalism of the 20th Century. But two world wars, the great depression, the Korean conflict, the Vietnam war, the civil rights movement and enormous medical advances made through animal research all worked to retard growth and activity in the American humane movement for more than half of the next century.

Abroad, at the turn of the century, new and angrier crusaders, such as Wagner and Schopenhauer, began adding their voices to the animal protection movement. Some began to worry that the new fervor for animals might be leading toward an altogether different end. *The Catholic Encyclopedia* of 1908 summarized a growing concern:

"While Catholic ethical doctrine insists upon merciful treatment of animals, it does not place kindness towards them on the same plane of duty as benevolence towards our fellow men. Nor does it approve of unduly magnifying to the neglect of higher duties our obligations concerning animals. Excessive fondness for them is no sure index of moral worth; it may be carried to un-Christian excesses; and it can coexist with grave laxity in far more important matters. There are many imitators of Schopenhauer who loved his dog and hated his kind." ✠

# CHAPTER 3. Nazi Germany: The Distortion of the Movement

*Even the German people would never have voted for the Nazis if they had known what they intended to do.*

Joseph Goebbels (Adolph Hitler's Minister of Propaganda and Enlightenment)

*Man should not feel so superior to animals. He has no reason to.*

Adolph Hitler

The modern day religions of environmentalism and animal worship are sometimes compared to ancient cults; they are, however more directly rooted in events and changes of recent centuries. New scientific discoveries and technological advancements brought longer life and greater material wealth for the masses, but the corollary shattering of age-old creeds and the relentless erosion of Medieval Christianity meant loss of meaning for much of humanity: as mysteries of life were unveiled by scientific inquiry, the certainties of previously held dogmas were no longer possible. Nihilism—the belief that yesterday's values no longer have meaning, that current institutions no longer serve— swept Europe.

Further, industrialization and urbanization began the separation of people from the natural world which even today makes many people feel rootless, displaced, isolated and anonymous. This loss of meaning fueled a new perspective which caused people to romanticize the natural world and to project onto animals the anxieties they themselves were feeling; namely, that they were victims of a heartless industrial age created by greedy, evil people who, if not stopped, would destroy all of the earth. As Ingrid Newkirk, one modern day prophet of this doomsday religion, would say 50 years after the holocaust: Humans have "grown like a cancer. We're the biggest blight on the face of the earth."

In war-leveled, economically devastated Germany, Nazism exploited the pain of the times by providing new meaning, scapegoats, a unifying goal, and symbolism for the coming *return to Eden*. We were taught that the ultimate Nazi goal was world dominance to be administered by a so-called German master race and recall with horror the human scapegoats of Auschwitz and Buchenwald. Many of us, however, never learned that the rallying symbols chosen to represent and romanticize the lost natural world—soon to be reclaimed for the Aryan race—were animals.

Adolph Hitler was apparently aware of the same relationship between man and animal praised by St. Francis of Assisi: "...Daily we make use of them and cannot live without them." But, instead of praising it, Hitler chose to exploit the relationship in very specific ways. The choice to exploit the animal issue rather than serve it is still with us today; a recognizable component of the modern animal rights industry.

As the Nazis came to power, animal protection laws catapulted onto the German legislative agenda. In 10 years under Nazism, more animal protection legislation was passed than during the preceding 50 years. First, laws regulating the slaughter of animals were passed which took sharp aim at the kosher slaughter practices of Jews. Soon thereafter, Hermann Goering announced that Germany would be the first of civilized nations to give rights to animals—rights that would remove them from the status of mere property. Through the new animal protection laws, animals would no longer have to suffer under the torment and torture of *vivisection*. It's interesting to note that the term *vivisection* was used interchangeably at the time to mean dispassionate analysis, synonymous in the German mind with the practice of Judaism, which was stereotyped as being hierarchical, reductionistic, mechanistic and devoid of proper animal instinct or emotionality.

Nazism brought to the animal issue a level of emotionalism and anti-rationalism only equaled by the modern animal protection movement. Nazism was a religion as well as a political system and the Goebbel's *Diaries* show that it reflected Hitler's personal religious views perfectly: "The Fuhrer is deeply religious, though completely anti-Christian. He views Christianity as a symptom of decay. Rightly so. It is a branch of the Jewish race. This can be seen in the similarity of religious rites. Both (Judaism and Christianity) have no point of contact to the animal element, and thus, in the end they will be destroyed. The Fuhrer is a convicted vegetarian, on principle. His arguments cannot be refuted on any serious basis. They are totally unanswerable. He has little regard for homo sapiens. Man should not feel so superior to animals. He has no reason to."

Endangered species and habitat protection became the focus of another set of Nazi laws that had the potential of regulating human actions in relationship to the natural world, far beyond the traditional controls placed in the social community. Every human action could thereby fall under control of the state. Hitler and Goering claimed to be setting a new worldwide humanitarian tone in compassion for animals. What emerged more clearly from application of the new laws, however, was that minor crimes could now be punished by death, while violent crimes against people and property often went unpunished. Hitler maintained the legal system of the old Weimar Republic, but instructed that in determining the severity of a given punishment, the fundamental idea behind a given crime should be taken into account. He was making certain that laws would be interpreted in light of the new religion of Nazism. Thus, vivisection, practiced from a different religious point of view, the dominion-oriented view, was punishable by a term in a concentration camp, while a violent crime against another human might go unpunished. Germany, in part through animal protection laws, was becoming a society in which punishment had less and less to do with the seriousness of the crime.

Nazi revisionists created a long Germanic history detailing close relationships with animals that supposedly once flourished in a society that was less anthropocentric and hierarchical, or dominion-oriented, than the Judeo-Christian heritage later foisted on Germany by foreigners. Germans were encouraged to reawaken in themselves their animal nature and to return to a pre-domestic state of spiritual communion with nature. (Priscilla Feral, long-time president of a Connecticut-based animal rights organization, Friends of Animals, adopted the last name *Feral* to signify a domesticated animal who has returned to the natural or wild state). Animal traits, especially predatory traits, were elevated. Hitler's nickname, *Wolf*, his *wolfhunde* dog and his *Wolf*

*Lair* headquarters demonstrate the systematic elevation of the predatory animal symbol to the level of cultural totem. Through the animal symbol and a rapidly developing Nazi mythology, Hitler sought to instill in German youth the predatory animal instincts which, according to the myth, had been destroyed by thousands of years of domestication and through mixing blood with the non-Aryan, subhumans which had once been slaves to the German people.

The Nazi system that replaced the old one didn't do away with hierarchical systems of relationships as they purported to do, but instead built two side-by-side hierarchical systems: one in which people were ranked from Aryans at the top to Jews at the bottom and another in which animals were ranked according to their popularity in Aryan mythological history. Pigs, according to the myths, were animals that the Jew "didn't understand." With Aryans they became popular creatures, indeed. Perhaps it is only coincidental that animal rights books and periodicals devote special time elevating the pig's characteristics relative to other animals or that Ingrid Newkirk was shown mugging with a pig recently in an *Los Angeles Times Magazine* interview or that with all the diverse targets available, rodeo queens, bull riders, beef aficionados, etc., it was Miss Pork who took a People for the Ethical Treatment of Animals pie in the face at the 1991 Iowa Pork Festival. While it may not be representative of any current anti-Semitism in the movement, it clearly shows a common philosophical source which is anti-Western ethic generally.

Nazism elevated the natural world, including animals, to a pedestal and then compared selected human traits with the traits assigned to animals. Aryans became aligned with the quickest, sharpest, most cunning and athletic, while the Jews, Gypsies, homosexuals and others they felt were undesirable were compared to rats, bedbugs, fleas and other vermin. When these two systems were put side by side, it was obvious that some animals were regarded more highly than some humans. Thus, by the systematic use of animal symbols, a blurring of the value of human life was accomplished.

Animals as mythological symbols are readily understood by people everywhere. They represent speed, cunning, sloth, filth, grace, wisdom, ferocity, beauty, athletic ability, virility, instinct—all of the elemental stuff of life. Hitler, master of the big lie and first to use mass disinformation as the basis for gaining and then holding power, used the animal symbol because it offered a connection to the natural world just distant enough so that it could be manipulated easily.

Using the Jewish people as scapegoats in combination with the use of the animal symbol accomplished the dehumanizing of the Jews by disconnecting them from the human community while firmly identifying them with animals that most people had an interest in exterminating. The systematic elevation of some animals concurrent with criticism of others enabled Goebbels to reflect, after driving through a ghetto: "These are no longer human beings, they are animals. For this reason our task is no longer humanitarian but surgical. Steps must be taken here, and they must be radical ones, make no mistake."

Vegetarianism in Nazi Germany became a sign of purity and eating meat became the symbol of decaying civilizations that still practiced dominionist attitudes over animals. Adolph Hitler, along with many of the elite Nazis, was a devout vegetarian who would not eat the flesh of the lower animals due to his feeling of spiritual kinship with them.

In addition, Adolph Hitler felt that Christianity, the step-child of Judaism, was doomed because it offered an improper relationship between humans and the rest of the animal world. Again, Nazism, with its mythic animal cult, offered the proper connection.

The Nazi cult, Hitler at the pulpit, held out the carrot of a future world purged of exploitative, dominionistic technology. It held out the vision of a pastoral world in which Aryans would peacefully commune with a replenished natural world while ruling other races of men. Who would have imagined that by elevating animals in relationship to people that the relative value of people would have decreased as well? Who could have foreseen that Hitler's statement that "man should not feel so superior to animals..." represented a warning that would finally lead to the annihilation of millions of human beings? Through the metaphysics of hate as practiced in Nazi/animalism, people were converted to sacrificial symbols of racial purification who, when killed, purged humanity of that part of man Nietzsche had warned we were tired of—rationality, the part that separates humans from other animals.

After the Holocaust, the romanticism of the animal cult lost its appeal to the masses. It bears remembering, though, that after the war Nazi youth, along with their screwy ideas about the equality of animals, grew up. They, along with their religion of animals and nature worship, have re-emerged throughout the western world whenever and wherever anarchist movements have operated. They are with us still, and so is the tendency to use animals as both symbolic and actual political tools.

A quick reflection on the dominant images of the Gulf War points clearly in this direction. In these days of fundamentalist environmentalism, the pictures of oil-soaked birds warn symbolically of environmental Armageddon reconnecting us to the earth through fear. Oil-soaked birds served the Gulf War quite literally as Willie Horton had served the 1988 presidential campaign; as a symbolic tool capable of generating public support through fear. In the ancient forests of the Pacific Northwest, the blurring is so great and the power of the animal symbol so important, many residents don't know whether the current old-growth timber debate revolves around trees or owls. The symbolic value of using animal images as political tools in connecting us to the natural world is shown, too, by the high cross-over vote of the so-called "Green" congressmen to animal rights issues.

While there is no evidence of Nazi ascendancy within the German Green movement today or in the past few decades, certain Nazi philosophical elements are present: Specifically, there is a yearning for communion with the pristine natural world, unspoiled by capitalism and industrialization. Replacing the power structure and de-industrializing society are key themes, along with hate. A number of Nazi veterans and former Hitler youth have been reported within the movement, along with many other diverse factions: feminists, Marxists, anti-nuclear activists, animal advocacy groups, anarchists and various ecologically minded interest groups. In this context, despite their political emergence as a political force in Germany in the late 70s, the Greens represent an ideological link from one period in history to the next when the animal symbol was skillfully exploited.

Postwar England became the next link, where, as David Henshaw of the BBC relates: "...[T]he truth was that England and European Fascism had long had a curiously greenish tinge to it...that was rather more than the fact that Hitler had been a serious vegetarian." In pre-World War II England after all, *The Fascist* magazine ran a front page cartoon showing an ox marked with the star of David, "congratulating an aged horse put out to grass; 'you will not be sent to hell on earth before you die. But neither Laws nor Animal Protection Societies can save us; they will cut our throats and let us bleed to death because they will not oppose the Jews who govern them.'"

In England, against this historical background where (amidst terrible cruelty to man and beast alike) the humane movement had been founded for both people and animals more than a hundred years before, it was formally hijacked and taken over by animal rights radicals. Their primary goal was no longer the humane treatment of animals, but rather, the promotion of radical social and political change, including the total abolition of human dominion—even to the exclusion of pet ownership. ⊞

# SECTION II

# THE HIJACKING

# CHAPTER 4. Organizations and Leaders

*Neither of us had ever been inordinately fond of dogs, cats or horses in the way that many people are. We didn't "love" animals.*
Peter Singer (speaking for himself and his wife), author of Animal Liberation
Bible of the Animal Rights Movement

*In a war you have to take up arms and people will get killed, and I can support that kind of action by petrol bombing and by bombs under cars, and probably, at a later stage, shooting of vivisectors on their doorsteps... It's a war and there is no other way you can stop vivisectors.*
Tim Daley, Animal Liberation Front

*He didn't like, he said, the idea of domestic 'pets;' if humans looked after animals, these should be regarded as 'refugees;' to call someone an 'animal lover,' was like calling him a 'nigger lover.'*
David Henshaw on Kim Stallwood while at the British Union for the Abolition of Vivisection before becoming executive director of PETA

## Background

The origins of the modern animal rights movement commences with the actions of two radical groups that mushroomed in the 1960s and 70s in England: the Hunt Saboteurs (HSA) and its militant offshoot, the Band of Mercy. The Bands of Mercy were originally formed as Humane Youth groups both in England and the United States, but this new group was destined to become the international terrorist organization, the Animal Liberation Front (ALF). Through these groups' actions, the British landscape transformed into a war zone in which animal zealots torched medical laboratories, firebombed fur-selling department stores, desecrated graves of long-dead hunters, and initiated attacks against gun and butcher shops. They targeted animals used in entertainment, too, and just displaying a circus poster was enough to put a shop owner's business in jeopardy.

The new groups took activism to higher levels by targeting *animal exploitation* as it was occurring. The younger generation was

—35—

tired of what it perceived as the lip-service orientation of the older, more traditional animal-protection organizations. They believed, like Mill during the previous century, that traditional organizations were too slow to condemn their own members' practices. But with Mill it wasn't so much he wanted the SPCAs to condemn anyone's practice as it was a matter of hypocrisy in his view to preserve their own habits while they condemned habits of the lower classes. This new crowd had no such vices—animal usage was now off-limits to the entire human race.

Prior to the new groups' formation, direct confrontation was not part of the humane movement's mode of operation. In the early days, the disruptions were strictly non-violent, personal protests, but it didn't stay non-violent for very long. The shift away from the traditional humane society mentality opened the door to a vigilante spirit that fed on itself, creating its own momentum and design. Soon, these groups increased their effectiveness by establishing liaisons with undesirable elements of society. This arrangement signaled a new and violent generation of protest activity and effectively launched the modern animal rights movement in England—15 years before Peter Singer's book gave a name to their cause.

The 20 years following the creation of HSA witnessed the evolution of a political force which carried confrontation beyond verbiage to property and business destruction, death threats, personal injury and attempted murder. While the movement claimed to have non-violent roots and invoked the names of Gandhi, Schweitzer and King, the physical toll of forced business closures and demolished property made a mockery of such statements. Actual deeds, and the oft-quoted observation by Ronnie Lee, founder of the Animal Liberation Front, that "Someday, someone will get a screwdriver in the face," underscored that the movement was based on terrorist enforcement and anticipated human injury in the process of liberating animals from exploitation.

The liaison with undesirable elements of organizing animal activist groups provided punch to terrorist threats and flexibility to segments of the membership who desired to do more than write letters. These advantages, coupled with the innocent-until-proven-guilty protections of a democratic society enabled activists to have it both ways. They could claim a non-violent intent to the world, while simultaneously supporting the most flagrant forms of violence to destroy an enemy. It became standard practice for the activist spokesperson to show an immediate and intimate awareness of events when issuing press releases, while at the same time disclaiming personal participation in a firebombing or any other illegality.

Although the connection may have been unmistakable, it was up to criminal forensics to prove and a court of law to convict. This form of tightrope walking enhanced the new activists' reputation with young people looking for new, daring causes. They brazenly danced in the face of authority while using the rules and protections for law-abiding citizens as a shield against criminal prosecution.

From the liaison with undesirable elements, activist groups discovered the advantage of working in loose affiliations within the general movement. To explain, this period of protest witnessed an evolving myriad of new organizations in support of animal activism: There were Christians for Animal Rights and Pagans for Animal Rights (whose deity, Gaia, just happened to promote the standard no meat, no leather, no factory farming animal rights). The new groups included right wing and anarchist groups which the previous antivivisection societies had not. ALF went from 30 to 250 members during the period 1976 to 1980, and up to 1,500 members by 1986. One of the most interesting of the new ALF members was Dave Nicholls who had previously been an organizer of the British neo-Nazis. In the past, he had led 80 skinheads through the streets of Colchester, "shouting 'seig heil' and giving Nazi salutes... and announced that 'blood will run in the gutter.'" By the mid-'80s there were more than 600 organizations and committees established to defend animals' rights. The reasons behind the formation of each new group in some cases had to do with location, in other cases, a specific objective; but the overall goal for all organizations remained unchanged: to end all animal exploitation. The range of support within an individual group ran from interest in pet-treatment issues to absolute prohibition of animal usage. Anarchist views tied the groups together.

This arrangement enabled violent activists to maintain multiple memberships in a bewildering array of groups and claim or disclaim association, depending on which direction the blame for any recent illegal activity happened to be drifting. In addition, a matrix of hard-core memberships could effectively control the general direction of a large number of such groups. Finally, such a dispersed arrangement, without any identifiable core group, provided anonymity for the true leadership of the movement.

Hardy put the situation in perspective: "Nineteenth century anarchists did not have to worry about providing spokesmen for the evening news, proper timing of press releases and coordination of press conferences in different media markets, direct-mail fundraising, distribution (preferably at charitable-organization postal rates)... or enabling supporters to conduct their contributions... To satisfy these mundane requirements... It followed in HSA's footsteps by forging links to parallel, aboveground organizations... The aboveground groups can fundraise, register for charitable exemption, mail national newsletters, and lobby, they can also distribute press releases for the underground group, stage press conferences, and deplore the excesses of their illicit counterpart even as they take advantage of their products, videotapes, photographs and lab notes."

Ronnie Lee was in law school in 1971 and was aware of the HSA. Lee and Cliff Goodman formed the Luton branch of the HSA and became regulars at upsetting hunting events. The avowed non-violent nature of the HSA, however, put Lee and his cohorts in danger of physical punishment by the huntsmen who were not sworn to non-violent retaliatory practices. It was clear to all that the HSA's tactics would only hinder, rather than stop the hunts.

Another group calling themselves the Angry Brigade departed from the non-violent sabotage methods of the HSA. Their actions included firebombings, which attracted intense media interest. In comparing the Luton group HSA activities, it didn't take long for Lee to grasp the advantage of actions that disrupted by outright destruction and that could occur without the risk of face-to-face confrontation. As a result, Lee and Goodman formed a new group called the Band of Mercy and started out on a burning mission of their own.

This approach accomplished a number of things for Lee that could not be reached through simple HSA activities. First, it did away with direct dialog. The actions of the Band of Mercy (and its successor, ALF) effectively denied discourse between the victims of the actions and the perpetrators. The refusal to negotiate or otherwise enter into any form of dialog or problem-solving with the target group blatantly stated the objective of animal activist work: that there was no alternative possible other than stopping what they believed to be animal exploitation. If the target was a butcher shop, the solution was to quit business. If the target was a department store with a fur section, the solution was to get rid of the fur salon. If the target was an animal research facility, the solution was to stop its work.

Lee and Goodman were both arrested and jailed in 1975 for vandalizing a research animal breeding farm. Their trial was the first public event for animal activists in England, complete with daily demonstrations and the creation of celebrity status for both Lee and Goodman. They received three-year sentences, during which Lee publicly stuck to his meatless diet (as had Ghandi in previous decades), getting out of prison early for good behavior in the spring of 1976.

Lee, upon release from jail, formed ALF and became the press officer for the group. Initially, about 30 members, ALF grew as it went on a concerted rampage of destruction over the next 10 years. Lee was sent to prison for another eight months in 1977 after being caught with mice from a breeding establishment in his home, but he avoided confinement thereafter until 1987, when he was sentenced to 10 years in prison. As of this writing, he is still incarcerated.

After Lee's second imprisonment, his care in planning activities increased tremendously. This stint in jail also resulted in the apparent diffusion of power in the movement. That is, the actual leadership, due to the numbers of new groups constantly popping up and the encouragement of individual action, was extremely hard to define. This mode of operation agreed with Lee's avowed anarchism, as he viewed order and struggle for political advantage as a distraction to the business of ending animal exploitation. His best plan was no plan, and his own organization was marked by its looseness.

Whether inside or outside prison, Lee has been regarded as the godfather of the animal rights activist movement in Britain. His future course remains to be seen, but Lee has not relented in his conviction that animal exploitation must be stopped. Once he gains freedom from prison, few people doubt that his dedication will remain as intense as it has been in the past.

The actions taken in England while ALF was leading the pack included firebombing buildings and vehicles, sending letter bombs to party leaders at Westminster (the Animal Rights Militia ARM signed off on this affair as they do when human life is risked because ALF publicly disavows physical violence toward people), perpetrating a poisoned candy bar hoax, coordinating raids across the country, firebombings of fur-selling department stores, and blowing up the Senate House at Bristol University. A grave desecration included smashing the headstone and removing the body of English folk hero and hunter, John Peel. Later, they notified the media that they had thrown his remains into a cesspit and left a stuffed fox head in the 123-year-old grave. The grave of the Duke of Beaufort, another hunter, was dug up in 1984 for similar reasons. Although ALF failed in its mission, it notified the press that it planned to mail the duke's head to Princess Anne. A month after the Bristol University explosion, bombs were left in trash cans outside Mcdonald's restaurants while they were filled with customers (they were located and dismantled). Vivisectors' cars were bombed and hunters were beaten in their homes. By 1986, acts of vandalism and sabotage had reached a rate of 40 per week. The economic sabotage of Mars U.K., which consisted of publicizing a claim of poisoned candy bars, cost Mars U.K. three million pounds in 1984. Debenhams department store in Luton lost nine million pounds in store destruction when firebombing was used to protest its continued sale of furs.

This period also witnessed the birth of many media efforts sponsored by animal activist groups, along with extensive growth in media sophistication. Their own presses not only propagandized to interested members, but also became a resource of information and propaganda for the mainstream media, which eventually grew into a fundraising conduit as well. Old time animal protection organizations were falling more and more under the authority of militant memberships. By the early '80s in England, all of the major animal welfare organizations were operating under subversive take-over attempts by members of the direct action groups. Alex Pacheco, who would soon co-found People for the Ethical Treatment of Animals with Ingrid Newkirk, visited England and met Stallwood during this pivotal period of the animal rights movement. A few years later, Stallwood came to the United States to become PETA's executive director.

Ironically, the British Union for the Abolition of Vivisection (BUAV), founded by Francis Power Cobbe in 1898 as a breakaway, radical alternative to the slower going National Anti-Vivisection Society, became the classic model for radical takeover. It had a large treasury and a sleepy membership whose numbers were steadily declining. Takeover efforts transpired over a 10-year period of membership infiltration, but the actual changing of the guard happened during a two-year period from about 1978 to 1980. Richard Ryder, who had collaborated with Peter Singer in the early to mid-'70s on developing animal rights theories, was in the forefront of the first wave of radicals. Stallwood popped up in the hierarchy of animal activism during the second wave of the BUAV takeover.

Kim Stallwood had joined the BUAV along with a wave of activists who were intent on taking control of the organization. He worked his way into the position of co-editing its bi-monthly publication and ultimately gained control of the entire organization. It is noteworthy that his media-liaison position also fit in with standard activist business. That is, he was able to serve as the information focal point for the organization, yet hide personal responsibility for anything behind his representative status. The positions he expressed to the outside media never had to be his own, but could always be issued in the name of the organization. As far as the outside world was able to determine, the power of the group could have been Stallwood himself or any other individual or number of members who chose to take on that role. This convention served Lee's ALF, Stallwood's BUAV and other animal activist organizations well, as it simultaneously kept selected portions of the public romanced and the authorities off balance.

Stallwood appeared to be more drawn to political influence than devotion to animals (as compared to Lee's fanatical devotion to animals and anarchy). Like Singer and several other movement founders, he made no claims for liking animals in the sense that some people did. And he didn't like the idea of people keeping domestic pets unless they were (as Ingrid Newkirk would later agree) refugees. Like Singer, he thought animals were the next natural benefactor of the evolving Western liberal tradition and that the extension of natural rights to animals should be the next step in the great trek from the Magna Carta through racial and sexual equality, which only recently had culminated in rights for endangered species in America. Kim said that calling someone an "animal lover," therefore, represented the same moral decadence as calling someone a "nigger lover."

He recognized that in an age of environmental passion, animals represented a potentially powerful vehicle for forging political alliances. Saving the planet had become such an overriding value for society that very few people cared that it was technically impossible to give rights to the environment and animals. Even if someone had sincerely wanted to dole out rights to animals, animals couldn't enter into our system without agents—being voiceless, they needed someone to speak for them. Stallwood believed that courting the new left was one of the avenues to success in building an activist coalition capable of such agency. By using feminists, environmentalists, new agers, gays and others, he was able to hobnob with diverse groups for political purposes, and could consistently exploit common interests.

His knack served well in the areas of media manipulation and political strategy. Both skills were apparent from his initial BUAV membership to his 1985 consolidation of power in the organization. He had been a BUAV member long enough before the 1978-1980 takeover period to have reached the position of *Liberator* editor. He controlled the nerve center of the outfit and continuously worked to solidify his position and politically expand his network. When ALF lost the cooperation of the Peace News Collective, Stallwood was perceptive enough to appreciate the political weight of ALF, and he offered BUAV office space to Lee. The previously sedate BUAV grew in notoriety for this association, and the internal balance of power was disturbed by two charismatic figures under the same roof. The old guard had been outnumbered since 1980, and the ultimate new power-and-control issue came to a head in 1985.

The annual meeting where this occurred brought together a curious blend of old-time members who supported the new animal rights activism as well as old-time members who held more traditional views. In addition to these factions, ALF and Stallwood's forces and others were fighting for control of the organization and its substantial treasury. Some of the new activist factions viewed the old guard as a disgusting stumbling block to any kind of progress at all.

The once staid, century-old BUAV found itself a carcass of sorts, over which the newer factions fought for remains. The annual meeting became an arena in which the "menopausal old bitches" found influence and control wrenched completely away from them and where shouts of "Fuck the rich!" became a battle cry of the new order. The meeting destroyed any remnants of the old order of power. The only dispute emerging from the meeting was who, among factions which either sympathized with, approved of, or indulged in illegal actions to reach their goals, would rule the roost. Ronnie Lee and Stallwood were opponents in this struggle.

That Stallwood came out on top is a tribute to his political strategist capability more than the result of any clearly expressed ideological position or leadership charisma. Politically, he could best be characterized as favoring "whatever works," and was better than Lee at staying out of the line of fire, and out of jail.

After failing in an effort to infiltrate and take over the RSPCA in 1986, Stallwood left the country and joined Alex Pacheco and Ingrid Newkirk in building PETA. It's important to note that Stallwood's excuse, when caught by RSPCA officials in a bogus membership drive, was that although laws or rules might have been broken in the takeover effort, the most important law for all to observe was the "higher moral law," which held that regardless of what actual laws prescribe, animals must live free from exploitation. This higher-moral-law refrain is interwoven throughout animal rights efforts around the globe whenever the rules of civilized society run counter to the immediate interests of animal rightists. Stallwood's mitigating claim didn't work. The RSPCA remained intact. Kim left the country.

The importance of the Lee and Stallwood background information lies in the fact that the export of ALF and Stallwood to the United States combined the British state of the art expertise for charity takeovers, media and fundraising, and political maneuvering that takes advantage of all levels of support from fanatics' assistance through celebrity endorsements.

It's clear that England set the modus operandi of the worldwide animal rights movement. It was in England where the takeover of humane organizations through radical means and covert infiltration were first used to gain public credibility and access to large treasuries. It was England where corporate raiding of non-profit organizations was perfected to a science. It is also the first place where economic sabotage, direct-action firebombs, letter bombs and high-tech plastic explosives were employed to stop animal usage.

In England, media sensationalism showing graphic portrayals of animal abuse, often contrived or augmented and known collectively as animal pornography, was combined with the distortion of facts and statistics to win sympathy for criminal acts and to serve as springboards for more fundraising exploitation. It is precisely this version of animal rights, as practiced and field-tested in England, that made Scotland Yard create a specialist animal rights squad in 1984. This same version was later exported with precision to the United States, where in 1989, the FBI was also forced to track ALF as a terrorist organization.

The rising tempo of activity in English animal rights also spilled into the rest of Europe and other parts of the world. In 1986 and the spring of 1987, attacks against meat, fur and research industries were recorded for the first time in France, West Germany, Sweden, Holland, Ireland, Spain, Italy and Australia. In May 1987, ALF members raided Bochum University in West Germany and removed eight rabbits worth $50,000 each, which had been selectively bred and monitored for advanced medical research.

With this track record, it's easier to understand why the selected methods of change favor deception, coercion, half-truth and uncompromising, cult-like tenacity. In the animalist view, civilization does not do "what it should" and would not voluntarily or democratically choose to adopt the animal activist line. Dr. Michael Fox of HSUS pinpoints the blame: "It is human nature that is the problem, and the suffering of the animal kingdom and the destruction of the natural world under our inhumane dominion are symptomatic consequences." Therefore, to Ronnie Lee and animalists everywhere, it is clear that the rest of the world must be dragged, kicking and screaming, or terrorized, into the realization that humans should live separately from and equally with animals.

## America: Finding Fertile Ground

*I don't use the word 'pet.' I think it's speciesist language. I prefer 'companion animal.' For one thing, we would no longer allow breeding... If people had companion animals in their homes, those animals would have to be refugees from the animal shelters and the streets. You should have a protective relationship with them just as you would with an orphaned child. But as the surplus of cats and dogs (artificially engineered by centuries of forced breeding) declined, eventually companion animals would be phased out, and we would return to a more symbiotic relationship—enjoyment at a distance.*

Ingrid Newkirk, Co-Founder of PETA

*I don't approve of the use of animals for any purpose that involves touching them— caging them.*

Dr. Neal Barnard, President, Physician's Committee for Responsible Medicine (PCRM)

*We don't want cleaner cages; we want empty cages.*

Tom Regan, Animal Rights Leader

Terrorist tactics did not come from England without accompanying ideals and a philosophy to drive them. However, it was not until 1975 when Australian philosopher Peter Singer wrote his book, *Animal Liberation*, that the entire animal rights world received its popular mission statement. His book gave the activists a simple, rational argument to support their beliefs. It also gave intellectuals a basis from which civilized debate could proceed. Of special interest is Singer's popularization of the term speciesism, which animal rightists use to indicate racism against species other than one's own, and which Singer claims is immoral and indefensible. Simply put, the main tenet of *Animal Liberation* is: "If you wouldn't do it to a human, you shouldn't do it to an animal."

Singer, though a late-comer to the movement, is one of the so-called "Oxford ethical vegetarians," a group that is credited collectively with founding the modern animal rights movement. Another of this group, Richard Ryder, was a key figure at the British Union for the Abolition of Vivisection during its years of turmoil and takeover.

Singer influenced Americans through *Animal Liberation* and his teaching position at New York University. He used the book and his profession as a platform for the promotion of animal rights theories to students at NYU and at a score of other colleges. He gave up his visiting professorship to go back to England and Australia, but has returned to the U.S. to lecture audiences on animal rights. His influence, through contacts with universities and through his books, *Animal Liberation, Democracy and Disobedience,* and *Should the Baby Live?*, has been enormous.

When the animal rights movement came from England, several elements worked together to legitimize and popularize the movement here. First, with the war in Vietnam over, young people were ripe for new causes. Next, the environmental movement linked animal protection with other already popular ecological causes such as saving whales, dolphins and the habitat. Singer's book articulated the cause, giving adherents an argument to support whatever actions they chose to use. Established social movements of the day supplied rhetoric for idealistic young people.

When Alex Pacheco arrived on the scene, he provided a link between the '70s and the '80s, environmental causes and animal rights extremism, and England even more closely with the North American continent. After converting to vegetarianism in the late 70s, Pacheco set sail on the *Sea Shepherd* the summer it was reported to have rammed a Portuguese whaling vessel. Adventures on such vessels were part of a rite of passage for devotees of environmental and animal extremist causes and some of the crews actually paid the captain to be part of the historical moment. Significantly, by this time in the progression of the movement, the *Sea Shepherd* had been purchased by Cleveland Amory's American group, Fund for Animals, and was piloted by ex-Greenpeace director, Paul Watson.

Amory's Fund for Animals has been a major player in the American animal rights movement from the beginning. The organization raises money and ostensibly directs it toward domestic and wildlife protection issues ranging from hunting to protecting whales to protesting biology class dissections. The Fund for Animals maintains the Black Beauty ranch/sanctuary for horses and other animals, publishes a magazine and a spay/neuter legislation bulletin. Kim Sturla, the promoter of pet-breeding bans in recent years is the Fund's Western Director. Amory's past associations and activities include, the New England Antivivisection Society, the National Society for Animal Welfare, and the World Federation for the Protection of Animals.

His Fund for Animals organization arose out of his expressed concern for animals, and originally from his disgust upon witnessing a bullfight. Amory relates that he reacted to watching the bulls being killed by throwing a wet stadium cushion at a victorious matador, catching him "just below the ear," and knocking him off his feet. This vigorous reaction is in keeping with one of the basic underpinnings of the animal rights movement. The significant differences between Amory's adventure and most animal rights illegality is that he performed in broad daylight in a crowd and now publicly recounts his act.

A second principle of the animal rights industry is revealed by Amory's additional comment that some time after the bullfighting incident, when writing about animal suffering issues, he discovered that "people sent in money."

Money, connections, influence and power are all rolled up into Fund for Animals activities. Amory's media background in journalism, book writing, radio commentary and TV appearances combine as a powerful resource for his cause. If Amory's major area of interest is animal protection fundraising, his minor study has been identifying sources of information, power, and influence across the country. Anyone with enough dash and desire to consort with such forces knows whom to go to for connections. The sanctuary/ranch was scandalized in recent years by news reports that its manager was quietly selling animals off the property for slaughter. Amory's stature in the movement is not as high as it could be in eyes of some of the younger zealots however, because of the scandal and because he's not a vegetarian. Nonetheless, Amory has obviously been an important conduit for new members coming into the movement and for media related connections.

Alex Pacheco went to England on the Fund for Animals ship and returned home full of new ideas. He had just turned 20 and, although he had expressed interests in becoming an FBI agent or entering the priesthood, he entered an environmental studies program at George Washington University in Washington, D.C. He was apparently more drawn to direct participation in the animal rights movement than textbooks, however, because after meeting Ingrid Newkirk in 1980, he scraped $60 together and started People for the Ethical Treatment of Animals (PETA) in his basement apartment.

PETA is the highest profile national animal rights organization in the United States today. The Humane Society of the United States may have more money (earning nearly $20 million annually in recent years) because it has retained its appearance of mainstream respectability and has in its name the legitimizing word, humane, but PETA gets far more publicity than HSUS. No one confuses PETA with an animal welfare organization anymore.

PETA claims up to 350,000 supporters by some accounts, but the actual controlling corporate membership consists of three people: Alex Pacheco, Ingrid Newkirk and Betsy Swart. People who consider themselves members will argue that the larger membership figure is valid, but the fact is, so-called members are merely paid-up supporters since PETA amended its certificate of incorporation on March 12, 1987, to read:

RESOLVED, That the Certificate of Incorporation of this corporation be amended by changing that Article designated as "SEVENTH" so that, as amended, said Article shall now read in its entirety as follows:

SEVENTH: The names and addresses of the members of the Corporation are as follows [It then lists the names of Ingrid Newkirk, Alex Pacheco and Susan Brebner and their respective addresses and continues]

The members of the Corporation shall also be the exclusive directors thereof. New members of the Corporation, if any, shall be nominated and elected by the Board of Directors based on the affirmative vote of two-thirds or more…

The power to adopt, amend or repeal the by-laws of the Corporation may be exercised by the Board of Directors of the Corporation upon the affirmative vote of two-thirds or more.

The direction and management of the affairs of the Corporation, and the control and disposition of its property and funds shall be vested exclusively in the Corporation's Board of Directors...

Hence, for purposes of power, budget and decision making, PETA is a three-member organization. It is noteworthy that Kim Stallwood arrived from England in late 1986 to take on executive director duties for PETA. In view of the humane movement's version of corporate raiding that occurred in England prior to his departure, the change in PETA's incorporation looks timely. Pacheco and Newkirk have been with the organization since its beginning in 1980; Swart replaced Sue Brebner as corporate secretary after Brebner (leader of spin-off organization, National Association of Nurses Against Vivisection) had served about 10 years in that position. Sue Brebner is now head of PETA's education department.

The corporation amendment protected PETA from takeover and also placed control of the radical agenda plus an enormous amount of charitable donations in the hands of three people.

This arrangement is important because it leaves PETA leaders free to maintain their aboveground appearance while acting as spokespeople for the terrorist organization ALF. As an example of how close this relationship can get, a film showing destruction during an ALF raid at the University of Arizona was transmitted via satellite from PETA headquarters within 24 hours of the break-in. Another revealing element of the association with ALF is that when Newkirk, Pacheco, Amory and many other prominent leaders across the country are directly asked about violence on behalf of animals, they refuse to unequivocally condemn it. A quote from USA Today serves as a perfect example of their style of equivocation: "I don't agree with any physical harm," says Newkirk, "But I... won't condemn it." This stands in sharp contrast to the movements of Gandhi and King, whose images are systematically and misleadingly borrowed for non-violence comparisons with the animal rights movement.

Additionally, PETA issues a several booklets and pamphlets that encourage subversive activities. One, called Activism and the Law counsels that, "while the decision to undertake 'illegal actions' may be unpopular, 'no struggle against exploitation has been won without them.'" The pamphlet also makes it clear that the "discredited" laws PETA's activists may disobey are not just municipal ordinances against sit-ins, but also statutes prohibiting burglary, arson, and grand larceny: "... [T]oday's legal system is a nightmare for the police officer: a poker game in which all the best cards seem to be in the defendant's hand," since "judges dismiss cases for cryptic, technical reasons."

PETA's Newkirk was born in England, spent nine years in a Catholic convent school while her father pursued his engineering career in New Delhi, and then emigrated with her family to the United States. Newkirk married race car driver Steve Newkirk, settled in Poolesville, Maryland, where she pursued a career in the stock market.

Her ambitions took a momentous turn in 1970, however, when she took a job as a kennel helper at the Montgomery County Animal Shelter. She also worked as a deputy sheriff and animal cruelty investigator. In 1978, she took the position of division chief for the county health department and wound up overseeing the Washington shelter. In 1980, her marriage to Steve Newkirk ended. Later that same year, she co-founded PETA.

To keep attention focused and funds flowing, she operates PETA as a kind of publicity show that serves as a constant source of news/entertainment and as a platform for fundraising. By her own admission, "Probably everything we do is a publicity stunt."

One of PETA's more memorable publicity stunts was an ad PETA ran in the Des Moines Register that compared the meat-eating American public with the cannibalism of convicted serial killer, Jeffrey Dahmer: The recommendation at the end of the ad read: "If this leaves a bad taste in your mouth, become a vegetarian." Newkirk has been credited for uttering some of the most radical statements by anyone in the movement. Among her most outrageous are: "Six million people died in concentration camps, but six billion broiler chickens will die this year in slaughter houses." With regard to animal testing, she responded that even if animal tests produced a cure for AIDS, "we'd be against it." Pet ownership, she said, is an "absolutely abysmal situation brought about by human manipulation."

Other stunts include: the distribution of veggie-burgers by activists in Moscow; airline flights for saved restaurant lobsters to Portland, Maine, for sea release; picketing; protests;

demonstrations; car smashing at auto dealerships to protest the use of animals in safety tests; and, disruptions of events such as the Hegins Pennsylvania pigeon shoot. All these things get PETA's name in the news and Newkirk's face in the media.

As mentioned earlier, PETA serves as public relations coordinator for the Animal Liberation Front and issues news releases that include sensational, emotionally upsetting images that are hard to forget. PETA turns the videotapes of such raids into fundraisers after editing them to show what it believes are the important elements. It also markets them as representations of the horrors that go on within labs. In one such tape stolen from the University of Pennsylvania in 1984, PETA reduced 60 hours of tape to 26 minutes. What remains of the videotape after editing portrays the researchers as sadistic. Bobby Berosini (see Ch. 8) won a unanimous verdict against PETA in his defamation suit against them that required the jury to find that PETA had knowingly, willfully and maliciously made false statements against him. In this case, a video showing Berosini in a bad light was found to have been altered. In the laboratory case, also covered later in this book (see Ch. 7), Alex Pacheco admitted that he had staged two photos.

Newkirk's current power stems in part from her marketable eccentric views, her quick mind and tongue at public appearances and in interviews, her accessibility to the press, PETA's unusual ability to issue press releases immediately after ALF raids, PETA's similarly unusual ability to produce copies of materials stolen during ALF raids, and PETA's absolute control of an $8-10 million budget which is used for everything from direct-mail fundraising to contributing money for defense of ALF members, to funding staff positions in like-minded organizations.

In a manner similar to the proliferation of animal groups in England, the American movement continuously spawns niche groups and spin-offs which share the philosophy but carry out specific, legitimizing or otherwise supportive activities. In light of spin-offs and the multiplicity of animal rights organizations, it is worth noting that many prominent figures are affiliated with multiple animal rights groups. Betsy Swart, PETA's secretary is also affiliated with Friends of Animals and In Defense of Animals; Susan Brebner who heads up education at PETA is in charge of National Association of Nurses Against Vivisection; Dr. Neal

Barnard, (who maintained a desk at PETA headquarters in earlier years), leads the Physicians Committee for Responsible Medicine and serves as a director on the board of New England Antivivisection Society (along with fellow NEAVS board members Amory, Newkirk and Pacheco. This cross-over pattern is common throughout the movement.

The name of the game, as in the British experience, is to create at least nine other spin-off, support or front organizations and to join as many organizations as possible. Each one is used to legitimize the next and all are used to legitimize animal rights philosophy in general by creating the appearance of an enormous groundswell of diverse, popular support. These groups provide a continuous flow of animal rights propaganda while hiding connections, actual power, and manipulating the media and interest groups.

The role of Physicians Committee for Responsible Medicine (PCRM), headed by Dr. Neal Barnard, is to serve as the movement's medical legitimizing agent. In this role, PCRM has repeatedly gained national attention for its proposed revision of the basic food groups to exclude meat. The new, basic food groups PCRM promotes are grains, legumes, fruits, and vegetables. More recently, PCRM gained media attention by warning the American public about the dangers of drinking milk, citing a study that included people already known to have an aversion to it. PCRM is also used as a resource for news and talk radio shows to argue against the use of animals in research. During these interviews, Dr. Barnard may not mention the fact that he is an animal rights extremist and doesn't believe in using animals for any purpose where they have to be touched or caged. Reporters working on medical or animal rights controversies who need a dramatic statement can always go to PCRM to obtain a quote to convey the message that even medical doctors are concerned about unnecessary, useless, unwarranted, unethical, or redundant animal research and experimentation. The American Medical Association censured the PCRM on July 26, 1990, for misrepresenting animal research and for implying that physicians who support animal research are irresponsible. The closing paragraph of that censure reads: "In Response to a Resolution passed unanimously at the recent AMA House of Delegates meeting, the American Medical Association calls upon the Physicians Committee for Responsible

Medicine to immediately terminate the inappropriate and unethical tactics your organization uses to manipulate public opinion. The Physicians Committee for Responsible Medicine does not represent a substantive body of physicians and your promotional materials and public statements should so indicate. We urge an immediate change in your tactics and strategies."

Nonetheless, the PCRM continues to fill a news/entertainment niche: it's a "credentialed counterpoint" for news reporters who want the right kind of zing or slant to their features. In fact, the overwhelming body of physicians (97 percent) understand the importance of animal research and subscribe to the rational application of such measures. By PCRM's own admission and despite its misleading name, less than 10 percent of PCRM's membership is made up of physicians, and AMA tallies based on PCRM's figures suggest that no more than .005 percent of American doctors are members.

Being a high profile animal rights legitimizer pays well. Internal Revenue Service 990 forms and court testimony show that PCRM has received $1,042,954 from NEAVS and PETA since 1987. Dr. Bernard serves as a medical and scientific advisor to PETA, and is also associated with PETA members through his service on the board of the New England Antivivisection Society which underwent a hostile taken over by a PETA slate in 1987. Alex Pacheco, Ingrid Newkirk and, as noted above, Cleveland Amory have all served on the NEAVS board.

Another spin-off organization that advocates animal rights is the Association of Veterinarians for Animal Rights (AVAR). It is headed by Dr. Nedhim Buyukmihci, faculty member at the University of California, Davis Veterinary School. Dr. Buyukmihci (Dr. Ned to PETA, which regards him as their chief veterinary advisor) disagrees with the use of live animals in certain laboratory training for veterinary education. A few years ago, Dr. Buyukmihci translated those views into legal action against the university to help establish an understanding between the school and himself as to the limits of his first amendment free speech rights and the school's ability to set curriculum standards. Both sides claim victory in the settlement, which leaves Dr. Buyukmihci on the staff and the school in charge of setting their own curriculum requirements. AVAR is listed along with Fund for Animals and PCRM in Newkirk's book, *Save the Animals*.

Dr. Buyukmihci is married to Kim Sturla, the western director for Amory's group, the Fund for Animals. Sturla, before going to work for the Fund for Animals, worked as director of the Peninsula Humane Society in San Mateo, California, where she was a chief proponent of a radical, media-grabbing ordinance to ban pet breeding. This ordinance was promoted under the flag of ending the so-called pet overpopulation problem and has continued to provide a media bonanza for the animal rights movement since its initiation.

To grab the public's attention, barrels of dead shelter animals and public executions of animals were shown on television. Promoters advised the public, and dog and cat breeders in particular, that they were responsible for the deaths of these dogs and cats and said the killing had to stop. Next, the standard animal rights rhetoric began. Animal rightists wanted to know how breeders could breed their dogs and cats while others died in shelters. They claimed the dogs that breeders produced displaced shelter animals on a one-to-one basis. Breeders were immoral.

Statistics from the Peninsula Humane Society, which, according to the *San Mateo Times*, underwent a hostile takeover by extremists in 1985, showed that the actual numbers of dogs and cats handled in the shelter had been dropping steadily. In 1974, the shelter took in 42,965; by 1990, the number had dropped to 15,810, without any coercive legislation at all. Nor did the animal rightists mention that the largest number of animals included in the total were stray, often ownerless, free-breeding cats on whom the ordinance would have no effect. They didn't mention that despite increases in human population, the number of pets entering shelters nationally has dropped 50-70 percent over the last 20 years because people do care. The very people targeted, those who still deliberately breed dogs and cats, are among the people who care the most and work the hardest for pets in society. But, most of all, they didn't once mention that they didn't believe in pet ownership.

In San Mateo, the ordinance that finally arose from the chaos after more than a year of struggle between animal fanciers and the animal rights campaign was enacted in substantially modified form. The original proposal, however, was touted across the country as "the San Mateo model" and has served as a springboard for ordinance proposals, fundraising and issue distortion in more than 100 locations nationally.

The animal rights breeding-ban campaign launched in King County (Seattle, WA) by the extremely radical Progressive Animal Welfare Society (PAWS) with the help of Kim Sturla presented some macabre variations on the already bizarre theme started in San Mateo. Mitchell Fox, a PAWS spokesperson, set the tone for what became a very disturbing battle when he warned: "We are killing animals every night at 6 o'clock behind closed doors and we want very much to change that, to go public with it. We want to do this killing on the steps of city hall and in the parking lots of populated malls and in parks. We want people to see it because there is nothing like that experience." Participants wanting to attend the ordinance hearings were advised not to bring either animals or animal parts into the hearing rooms.

As with the English experience, the number of organizations and number of multiple memberships has grown dramatically here. The 1992 figures show more than 400 animal rights groups with 990 IRS forms displaying the total budgets for the 26 most active and visible animal protection, welfare and rights groups at $577 million. The number of Americans belonging to animal rights groups has grown to five times the total membership of 1984.

There are countless animal rights groups besides the ones mentioned above. What is true about the ones covered above, however, is true generally for the whole movement: it is tightly knit at the top; it is a top-down movement in terms of ideology, concept and forms of control; it is served by violence that its leaders refuse to condemn; it gives no quarter to opposing views; and, it has no limitations on means used to achieve desired ends. Kim Stallwood's tactic of using the new left to achieve political goals transplanted a proven strategic mode of operation to the American movement. This mode takes advantage of the opportunity to express any beliefs, no matter how unacceptable, in a civilized society while at the same time enjoying, and encouraging the support of, uncivilized, illegal and elusive enforcement agents.

They are tireless in working to effectively extend natural rights status to both animals and natural resources by regulating their usage away from humans and by removing them from the classification of private property. As revealed by Dr. Michael Fox, an enormous amount of energy is being applied to this end: "Dealing with institutionalized forms of inhumane animal exploitation takes teamwork and special expertise. The Humane Society of the United States employs lobbyists, scientists, attorneys, investigators, humane educators, fund raisers and support staff in this endeavor." Dr. Fox expresses a goal of nothing less than putting animals and nature on every agenda of public policy and private action. ⊞

# CHAPTER 5. Divide and Conquer

*It doesn't matter what is true...You are what the media define you to be. [Greenpeace] became a myth, and a myth-generating machine.*

As noted by Paul Watson, co-founder of Greenpeace

History documents that the goals of the radical element of the animal rights movement have been served by terrorism. Prominent leaders in the mainstream of the animal rights movement are not willing to appear pro-violence in public because they realize they must maintain credibility and respect to function within the social structure they need to influence. Some, however, have publicly expressed understanding of the feelings which could have led to violence and/or broken laws in animal rights actions. How do these leaders maintain working relationships with mainstream groups while infiltrating them with radical members? How do they maintain their communication and relationships with a terrorist network? There are a number of classic movement techniques that shed light on this question.

**Associating With Established Institutions.** First, let's look at linking up with the establishment. There are decided benefits in associating with acceptable institutions. By using traditional humane societies as forums to promote extremist positions, animal rights groups have been able to operate under a mantle of mainstream acceptability and respectability. This has enabled extremists to appear reasonable while promoting progressively more radical ideas.

Local humane societies operating around the country have experienced varying degrees of infiltration and radicalization by animal rights advocates. Most of these societies still promote the traditional animal welfare positions of responsible use and humane treatment of animals. But nearly all humane societies employ people whose personal levels of activism range from disinterest to passion. The attitudes of these employees determine the degree of standard practice or radicalization exhibited by the organization. When the majority of employees, or those in control, are radical, the entire organization takes a decidedly nontraditional approach to its humane mandate. Specifically, it adopts and promotes the animal rights philosophy.

To outsiders, a glimpse of what's happening at the local humane society may only be apparent at the annual benefit dinner. If vegetarian dishes are all that are offered, you can be fairly assured that the majority of people in control have fundamentalist views on the subject of animal rights. Another glimpse presents itself if overly strict or doctrinaire pet-adoption policies are operative. If existing policies prevent responsible people from adopting pets because their normal lifestyles don't meet with shelter policy, adoption policies may be based on animal rights philosophy rather than on a knowledge of an animal's needs.

The radical **Progressive Animal Welfare Society (PAWS)**, headquartered just north of Seattle, Washington, has policies of pet adoption that have disappointed seemingly responsible people who are told that their homes are considered poorer risks for pets than euthanasia. Information from all over the country suggests that philosophically based rejections occur at animal-rights-dominated shelters routinely. The national animal rights organizations, with one exception, do not shelter animals and it is the goal of animal-rights-oriented humane societies to eliminate that aspect of their responsibility at the first possible moment. They want to promote their philosophy of no pet ownership.

Animal-activist-controlled humane societies have started using radical publicity, sometimes referred to as hit pieces or animal pornography, to raise funds or sway public opinion on specific issues. The primary example of this is putting animals to sleep on television.

While the differences in traditional approaches and animal rights pursuits may be apparent to humane society members internally, the general public is often unable to distinguish between the rhetorical distortions of animal rights fundraising and those of traditional animal welfare fundraising (the more graphic the characterization of animal abuse, the easier it is to raise money).

The vast number of people working for animals at different levels allows the radicals to appear to be part of a continuum of interest rather than part of a highly organized and distinctly fanatical movement. Blurring the lines between traditional and radical humane societies also serves as the radicals' ticket to stay in the game, and it enables them to gradually change the entire playing field as well. The intent to infiltrate mainstream organizations, take them over, convert their status, influence and finances to an animal rights agenda, has been a field-tested practice since the early 70s.

Living in the most culturally diverse society in history, Americans work hard at being fair-minded, objective, reasonable, and politically correct when it comes to assessing minority or atypical points of view. It's part of the American character to want to err on the side of fairness. The layered effect of fully radicalized, partially radicalized and fully traditional humane societies provides a camouflage, protecting the too-outrageous-to-believe aspects of the movement from polite public discussion. By speaking out against the animal rights advocates, the traditional humane societies could paint at least part of their own operations with the same brush.

Furthermore, by placing themselves among and alongside members of the traditional humane movement, the radical elements attempt to legitimize pre-existing, less extreme points of view. This *radical flank effect* benefits both factions by continually moving the middle ground in the direction of radical change. It makes friendly companions of the more liberal elements of the traditional humane societies even if they don't openly support the extremists' goals.

Another radical flank effect tactic frequently used is that of animal rights advocates offering their own extreme view as opposition to the consensus position of the mainstream, while characterizing the mainstream as an opposite extreme. This establishes a playing field that assumes that two extremes are opposing one another, when in fact, the mainstream is already a midpoint consensus of public or professional opinion. The effect of being able to characterize the center as the other end of the teeter totter moves the entire issue into the extremists' territory. Hence, any movement that takes place is from the real mainstream center toward the extremist position. The mainstream, under these circumstances, has only the options of standing pat or allowing concessions. There is no opportunity to move further away from radical demands.

The continuum grows more populous as differences of opinion create splinter groups to provide a voice for specific concerns and to obliterate and displace the mainstream. In this manner, animal rights groups are following principles tested earlier English animal rights and environmental movements as they spawn more and more spin-off groups, thereby insulating and legitimizing the influence that causes radical flank effect. Former Sierra Club executive, David Brower, describes this technique: "I founded Friends of the Earth to make the Sierra Club look reasonable. Then I founded the Earth Island Institute to make Friends of the Earth look more reasonable. Earth First! now makes us look reasonable. We're still waiting for someone to come along and make Earth First! look reasonable."

The **Humane Society of the United States (HSUS)** is a nationally known organization that practices animal rights while collecting mainstream contributions from an unsuspecting public. It had already moved into the animal rights camp by the mid 80s, but even today most Americans think of it as a be-kind-to-pets organization. Dr. John McArdle, while director of lab-animal welfare at HSUS, advised HSUS delegates in 1984 never to use terms such as animal rights or antivivisection. Instead of using these alarming words, he recommended working against the source of animals used in research. In other words, getting people worked up over the possibility that their pets may wind up on a lab table would enhance the opportunity to restrict animal research. Fundraising from a pet-owning public, he might have added, is also easier if they think you're in favor of pet ownership. McArdle, now with the American Antivivisection Society, may have gone too far when he suggested that brain-dead humans should be substituted for animals in surgical research. "It may take people a while to get used to the idea, he said, *but* once they do the savings in animal lives will be substantial."

To demonstrate further where HSUS sits on the animal welfare/animal liberation spectrum, HSUS Vice President Michael W. Fox told *Newsweek* in 1988: "Humane care is simply sentimental, sympathetic patronage." More recently, a letter from President John Hoyt to HSUS supporters included the promotion of animal rights as one of the organization's goals. Other signs of the HSUS shift to an animal rights philosophy are demonstrated by its *Breakfast of Cruelty* campaign aimed at eliminating bacon and eggs as the all-American breakfast, and the *Until There are None Adopt One* campaign aimed at making animal shelters the politically correct place to get a pet until there are no more surplus animals.

The HSUS produces written material aimed at audiences ranging from children to adults that includes programming language and hidden agendas. The phrase, "we try to be kind, but most of our kindness is killing," is woven throughout the *Until There are None* literature. It's chilling to note the connection of the word kind with the word killing. The phrase appears five times throughout the literature and implants the message that kindness is killing, a particularly disturbing thought if combined with a belief system that values humans and animals equally.

A spin-off group, the National Association for Humane and Environmental Education, a youth division of HSUS, publishes *Kind News Jr.*, (Kids in Nature's Defense Club), for school children first through fifth grades. The newspaper carries features on animal facts, celebrities, puzzles, a question and answer column written by Dr. Kind, opportunities to join in petition drives, etc. An interesting aspect of the newspaper is the teachers' guide that accompanies it. For example, in one guide, short stories from the animal's viewpoint relate their lives as entertainers. Teachers are instructed to read the animals' accounts of their lives to the students and have them write happier stories for the animals; the animals in the sketches are depicted as upset, overworked, or beaten during the course of their entertainment lives. Children are then instructed to make a list of ways people can entertain themselves without using animals. The surface agenda of the newspaper is one most parents would approve. The hidden agenda is one of developing attitudes that support the animal rights philosophy.

For older children, the Youth Education Division of HSUS publishes a *Student Action Guide* designed to build on this foundation with targeted activities such as starting your own animal/environmental protection club, with suggested topics ranging from pet overpopulation to global warming.

Other in-school animal-rights-education projects sponsored by animal rights groups at both the national and local levels include requiring students to write letters of concern to radical animal rights and environmental groups, which can then be bundled up and sent to legislators to show how much the kids care about animals. Still other assignments have included writing on issues regarding experimental research, trapping, hunting, and euthanasia. Students are instructed to write about or debate an issue using only reason and facts and not to forget the question of morality.

Despite these deviations from traditional humane society concepts, the animal-welfare-oriented public remains naively supportive. The programs can be interpreted more than one way and HSUS naturally retains its traditional, legitimizing name.

**Exploiting a Public Misperception.** The animal rights radicals have seized on the idea that the number of shelter animals being destroyed by euthanasia can be sold to the public as proof that animal overpopulation is caused by the immorality and greed of dog and cat fanciers. This claim is made to a generally uninformed public in the face of heroic and successful efforts by fanciers over the last two decades to educate the public about how they can live with pets in an urban setting. In fact, dog and cat fanciers, through their clubs, are the bedrock elements of animal welfare in the United States.

Recent American Humane Association figures show a 45 percent drop in dog euthanasia from 1985-1990; yet rightists allege that overall numbers have never been higher, with purebreds comprising 25% of the total. These claims represent lies and half truths. Impoundments for all dogs, mixed and purebred, have been steadily decreasing for more than 20 years. As strays and random-bred dogs are removed from the landscape the only category of deliberately-bred dogs remaining - purebreds - inevitably represents a greater percentage of the total. But because adoptors prefer purebreds, their euthanasia rates are much lower than impoundment rates.

The animal rights groups continue to ignore the downward trend of euthanasia and continue to use overpopulation as a fundraising tactic. No one likes to hear that an innocent animal has to be killed because no one wants to adopt it. The optimum solution is that animal euthanasia will end. It is equated with suffering, and on a more subtle level is blamed on human dominion. These two themes reflect the overt and hidden agendas associated with the animal rights movement. On the surface, the goal is a fair, pain-free existence for animals that would not include euthanasia to control the human habitat or serve as a means of disposal for those who disown their pets. The underside is the proposition that animals should be left to live and die and procreate on their own, living a completely separate existence free from human meddling. This translates to no pets, animal agriculture, hunting, trapping, fishing, riding, chasing, and no assistance dogs for the blind, deaf, and developmentally disabled.

With regard to the current status of stray animals and unwanted pets, people are generally not aware of the reduction in euthanasia rates over the past 20 years. They are also unaware that the problem of overpopulation is moving toward its own resolution because people do care. When people made a shift to urban life, it became more complicated to own pets. The result was a large population of animal-purchasing Americans who dreamed of Old Yeller or Lassie, but who soon discovered that their needs and their pets' needs clashed.

The humane movement was ready when, in the '70s, people surrendered their pets to the shelters because they could not properly care for or no longer wanted the responsibilities of caring for a pet. They tackled a complex and daunting trend with excellent public education, assistance and problem-solving measures, often with little outside recognition and almost always on shoestring budgets. As people adjusted to the realities of a contemporary urban existence, awareness about pet ownership increased and the numbers of pets surrendered to shelters decreased.

However, the stage had been set for the animal rights movement to capitalize on the agony of euthanasia as a solution and the existence of a problem that will be with us as long as people can own pets. The statistics on euthanasia allowed the animal rights groups to mount a public campaign against breeders and the American Kennel Club. Through this campaign, they could raise money and take credit for any progress made.

What is really happening? Overpopulation is a mythological crisis. Using this term as the basis for current problems focuses attention away from problem solving, engages opposing sides in a rhetorical debate that seeks to fix blame, and urges an instant remedy instead of a long-term solution. Let's look at the data. According to *The Animals' Agenda* (October 1991), from 1985 to 1990, the nationwide euthanasia of dogs and cats dropped approximately 40 percent. American Humane Association figures show an approximate 45 percent decrease for dogs and a 27 percent decrease for cats. The number of unwanted pets may never reach zero. At the turn of the century in America, packs of wild dogs ran through the streets; people in their 40s or 50s may recall childhood memories of dogs running wild. Animal control agencies and shelters have done much to eliminate this problem.

The humane societies, which began by sheltering and protecting, have always relied on public support. In the beginning, the numbers of unwanted or unclaimed animals made it easy to gain sympathy and funds from the public. But now, with the decline in numbers of those who need to be protected, it is more difficult to get public attention. This gap in the need for support and the ability to attract support opened the door for animal rightists to enter with the short-term solution of fundraising around the issue of life or death, rather than simply shelter.

The euthanasia trend is downward today not because of any single answer or from the efforts of any single group of animal lovers, but because of numerous approaches being applied by a great number of humane and caring people. Efforts initiated by the dog community include public education programs, breed rescue programs, breeder contracts requiring spaying and neutering of pet-quality puppies, better stud-dog management, more emphasis on training classes and puppy kindergarten (the single most cause of dog abandonment is behavior problems), and public education programs.

**Professional Information Gathering and Fundraising.** Animal rights advocates have become professional in their approach to organization and strategy, which has taken the humane movement far beyond the traditional capabilities of most charitable animal organizations. Direct-mail solicitation has become so sophisticated that nonprofit animal rights organizations can select specific groups from the general public and play them off one against the other, fundraising from each for some causes and from all for others. Serious dog breeders may support pleas to eliminate puppy mills, while the general public may respond to appeals to eliminate all dog breeding and both groups may be solicited to prevent pet theft. If it takes more than one organization to promote mutually exclusive crusades, establishing a spin-off organization is simple and consistent with the animal rights strategy of having so many splinter groups moving in so many directions that no one can keep track of them all.

Mailing lists are organized not only to catalog donors' special humane interests, but solicitations also query respondents to find out whether they feel that illegal activities are justified if the aim is to rescue suffering animals. Positive responses to this type of inquiry, while not financially rewarding, produce contacts that could aid the covert side of the movement. For instance, a question on PETA's "National Referendum" mailer asks respondents: "Do you feel that peaceful yet illegal activities are ever justified when their aim is the rescue of suffering animals?" The answer choices range from "usually" to "never." The American Society for the Prevention of Cruelty to Animals (ASPCA) 1991 Animal Protection Survey was mailed with address labels affixed to the forms so that when returned respondents are identifiable by names and addresses. Questions seek responses regarding priorities as to lab testing with animals, fur trapping and ranching, factory farming, entertainment, hunting, fishing, and wild animals.

The question that tops them all, if you happen to be a recruiter for an underground organization, is this: "BREAK-INS AND SEIZURE: Laboratories experimenting on animals have been broken into, records confiscated, and animals removed, in an effort to call attention to poor living conditions and experiments that cause animal pain and suffering. Individuals wearing fur coats have been angrily confronted on the street, and in some instances stores selling furs have been vandalized. Where do you stand on the issue of using such tactics to protect the right animals have not to be abused?"

The ASPCA is asking a question and selling a viewpoint. The phrase, "...protect the right animals have..., " assumes that there is no question that animals have rights, regardless of the definition of the word abuse. The following are the multiple-choice answers:

a. Violence is always wrong.

b. Violence is not desirable, but it is permissible to damage property to save an animal's life.

c. Protecting animals from human cruelty requires whatever means are necessary.

If respondents mark the box next to answer (c), they fall within the parameters of the whatever-it-takes zealot list. These people are likely to contribute, regardless of their income as indicated by other demographic data, and if properly screened and recruited, some could be moved to translate their feelings into action.

PETA and ASPCA are not alone in this information-gathering activity, as other animal rights groups use questionnaires that seek attitudes and feelings about illegal activities. It doesn't take a lot of imagination to realize that several animal rights organizations all mailing their own questionnaires could gather an enormous amount of useful information. Sharing this information could produce explicit profiles for each contributor.

**Celebrity support.** The use of celebrities to promote the animal rights cause is another technique used by savvy leaders. Doris Day has founded her own animal rights organization, and celebrities such as Bob Barker, Candice Bergen, Paul and Linda McCartney, Tony La Russa, Loretta Swit, Rue McClannahan, Ed Asner, k.d. Lang, Kevin Nealin and Roger Caras have all been known to support animal rights causes.

Anyone who has ever tried to get a balanced view of animal issues on television soon learns that the radicals are sophisticated players who have been involved with the media for so long they have a built-in advantage. In addition, the movement has followers in the media who are not necessarily national celebrities, but rather are well known in their local markets. And because sensationalism sells, typical and positive stories about animals are not hot enough to be interesting. This combination has made it difficult for the mainstream viewpoint to be covered.

**Movement Publications.** Another type of media distortion commonly used by animal rights advocates is found in various publications issued to propagandize their own members. In *PETA News* outright distortions are systematically used, but in other publications the distortions may be more subtle. An article appearing in a Friends of Animals publication (Feb/Mar 1991 edition of *Actionline*) prints in bold type a subheading that immediately grabs the reader's attention: *Moyer's stages of successful social movements.* Upon noticing this subheading, one's eyes search for clues as to what this article is about and who Moyer's is. Straight-away, one sees "Bill Moyer," and a biographical description that could easily describe *the* Bill Moyers of television fame.

If you're an animal rights activist, having a person of Bill Moyers stature on your side would make you feel your cause was worthwhile. However, it is not Bill Moyers, but rather a Bill Moyer who is writing the article. Perhaps suggesting that the intention of the article is to make people leap to conclusions is unfair, but the people presented with this article in a test study first believed that Bill Moyer was the television personality, Bill Moyers.

In this article, which has no apparent title, the subject relates other successful social movements such as the civil rights movement with the animal rights movement. It's an impressive endorsement of animal rights especially if one mistakenly believes that it is coming from a public figure of Moyers' background and stature.

**Appropriating Established Causes.** The practice of appropriating the goals and rhetoric of other causes legitimizes the animal rights movement in the eyes of the public in a number of ways, and it is another clever technique. It allows the radicals to anoint themselves with the older movement's already-won social acceptability, which then enables them to appeal to the public as something decidedly different from what they are. Specifically, it allows them to confuse the animal rights advocates' radical goals with more mainstream positions. It also allows them to raid the older group's members and funding sources.

Specific examples of attempts to exploit other movements, to disguise their messages within the rhetoric of the other causes are: the civil rights movement; the feminist movement; the environmental movement; the Aquarian/new age/new world order devotees; and the vegetarians. There are also Jews for Animal Rights, Jehovah's Witnesses for Animal Rights and a long list of Christian denominations for Animal Rights.

**Civil rights movement**

Peter Singer, considered a founder of the modern animal rights cause, stressed in his book, *Animal Liberation,* that the oppression of animals must be compared to the tyranny of white humans over blacks. He titled his first chapter, *All Animals are Equal...or why supporters of liberation for Blacks and Women should support Animal Liberation too.* Animal rights propaganda is packed with descriptions comparing the lives of animals under human domination to slavery. This allows animal rights advocates to exploit the history of slavery, which strikes a responsive chord in most Americans. One antivivisection newsletter uses one of Dr. Martin Luther King Jr's famous speech refrains, "because no lie can live forever," to sell its no-research position which claims that animal experimentation is a medical and scientific fraud. Another common tactic is comparing lab-animal liberation to the underground railroad, as in the liberation of Dr. John Orem's experimental cats from Texas Tech University. In reality, the only animal rights connection to the civil rights movement is the systematic exploitation of it through the use of free-speech protection.

Suggestions that similarities exist between animal rights leaders and Dr. King are incredible. Dr. King's leadership was nonviolent. He didn't have a terrorist wing and he strongly condemned violence. He actually fought against tactics that were strikingly similar to those employed by the Animal Liberation Front.

The differences between animal rights leaders and Dr. King are glaring and the comparisons generated for the movement's aggrandizement boggle the mind. The same contorted comparisons are made with Mahatma Gandhi and Dr. Albert Schweitzer. Gandhi, like King, condemned violence. Their non-violence was not the animal rights movement's version of non-violence. And as for the comparisons with vegetarians, neither Gandhi nor Schweitzer come to mind as readily as more authoritarian or militaristic vegetarians of past world history.

**Feminist movement**

Feminist language has likewise been appropriated and incorporated into the animal rights cause. Ingrid Newkirk supports Peter Singer's position by claiming that: "Animal rights is a natural step for feminists: it's not just an extension of the struggle against domination and oppression, it's an integral part of it." Her argument relies on previous extensions of our ethical circle, but neglects to observe that an extension to animals would grant rights to a voiceless constituency for whom only the animal rightists are qualified to speak.

In an extensive exposé article in the *Animal Rights Agenda* called "The Club, The Yoke and the Leash...What We can Learn from the Way a Culture Treats Animals," the animal rights cause is reframed in feminist terms. Here we are told that the club strategy allows us to "kill animals for gain, sadistic pleasure and affirmation of manhood...domination through brute force." In the yoke stage we domesticate or enslave for our use; and in the leash phase, we dominate through deceit as in the master over pet arrangement. The article promotes the idea that hunting produces callousness and "that teaches men not to feel anything when they kill or maim a living creature."

Pornography in the form of bestiality is mentioned as a major club force, as is vivisection, in which animals are tortured in the name of science and in which the high priests of medicine learn to suppress their feelings and become insensitive. "Having proved themselves callous, insensitive and unfeeling and able to keep their mouths shut, because what goes on in the government-funded labs is kept secret from the taxpaying public patriarchy's future healers are deemed worthy of practicing their skills on people." The author claims: "Rape, especially gang rape, strikingly resembles hunting." Stalking and degrading the victim while enjoying the victim's terror are other similarities described.

During the yoke phase of domestication, castration and forced breeding occur. Rodeos are used as examples of modern-day re-enactments of attempts at subjugation and domestication. During the leash stage, pets apparently represent women who are mere tokens and who, unlike slaves, have no economic value to recommend themselves and, therefore, are disposed of at will.

A *Seattle Times* (12/1/91) feature titled "WSU [Washington State University] is a nerve center for growing 'ecofeminist' network," gives more perspective to the overlap of animal rights, environmental and feminist interests. In it, the editor of the *Ecofeminist Newsletter*, Noel Sturgeon, reports: "Women have always been connected with the earth both culturally and socially...Nature is often described as feminine fertile, nurturing and beautiful. Negatively, both are exploitable." In the same article, another feminist calls "ecofeminism the third stage of the women's movement after suffrage in the early part of the century and women's liberation in the 1960s and '70s. Michael Fox of HSUS, probably unaware of the percentage of his contributors who are women, has warned against the 'male, monotheistic religion of reason.'"

In the *Feminists for Animal Rights* newsletter (volume v, nos. 1 and 2, winter-spring 1990), interesting and little-known facts emerge: "Approximately 60,000,000 people could be adequately fed and saved if Americans reduced their intake of meat by 10%; the American meat-eating habit is the driving force behind the destruction of tropical rainforests. The production of excrement by U.S. livestock is 250,000 pounds per second. Later, a book, *The Sexual Politics of Meat*, by Carol Adams is promoted, in which reference is made to an apparent article starkly entitled, "Man as Fucker and Carnivore," March, 1988. The Feminists for Animal Rights describe themselves as vegetarian women with a vegan orientation. Most mainstream animal welfarists don't have the slightest idea of what this means.

**Environmental movement**

Environmentalism is another cause whose message animal rights advocates have appropriated and on which they piggy-back in the hope of gaining converts and funds. One of the distinguishing characteristics of the animal rights version practiced in America is its parasitic attachment to the popular environmental movement.

The chief value of jumping aboard the environmental movement came from the public's misperception that they were part of the popular movement that was saving the earth. Early on, many conservationists recognized these animal rights advocates as ignorant, media-created fundraising freeloaders. Alas, 10 years later most of the traditional conservationists/preservationists, like many of the mainstream animal welfarists today, had succumbed to the radical flank effect. Through this process, they were eventually seen as outside the new mainstream. They found themselves dated, trivial and useless to the new and improved movement.

The new humane and environmental movements were for true believers. Being totally doctrinaire and evangelical, they no longer require science, scientists or experts on any subject. Anyone who has ever tried to defeat legislation proposed and pushed by radicals in either the animal rights or the environmental movements knows that factually accurate and verifiable data is not always used. Going through the legislative process opposing any of these extremists has been dubbed "compulsory irrationality" by wise-use advocates.

**Outright Takeovers**

The New England Antivivisection Society and the Toronto Humane were taken over by PETA slates. They had respective treasuries of $8 million and $14 million, which made them attractive. After the takeover, an article in the *Globe and Mail* reported new membership criteria, which discriminated against professions deemed cruel to animals, such as pet breeders, trappers, and hunters.

In 1985, The *San Mateo Times* [California] reported a surprise coup at the Peninsula Humane Society. Like others that took a radical plunge in the 80s, it was one of the richest humane societies in the country. Following a takeover, this humane society led the nation by introducing a breeding moratorium ordinance that limited the right of people to breed their animals. The justification for this position by animal rights advocates is that it is improper to breed animals while others die in shelters. One must recall the national level HSUS campaign, "Until There are None Adopt One," to grasp that these are highly organized nationwide campaigns. A commonly asked question about the animal rights movement, its takeovers and its priorities is whether the radical rhetoric is all just smoke to generate money.

The following correspondence between a traditional Peninsula Humane Society member and a new, radical, acting director casts light on the issue and gives unique insight as to the movement's frame of mind:

10 Stadler Drive
Woodside, CA 94062
12 July 1988

Mr. Michael S. McFarland, Executive Director
Peninsula Humane Society
12 Airport Boulevard
San Mateo, CA 94401

Dear Mr. McFarland:

I have your letter inquiring why I have not renewed my membership in PHS, and it deserves an answer.

My wife and I are long-time pet-lovers, and we have been active in Newfoundland dog activities for more than two decades. In particular, I have taken leadership roles in establishing the rescue services of both the Newfoundland Club of Northern California and the Newfoundland Club of America, of which I served as President for several years. It is perhaps needless to say that my wife and I share the goals to which I have assumed PHS was dedicated — the welfare of animals through rescue, direct intervention, neutering, public education, and the like.

Unfortunately, we have been dismayed by recent directions taken by PHS, as evidenced by the course-and-meeting booklets we have received in the mail. Some of the courses lie obviously within the scope of PHS's mission; e.g., volunteer training and child education. But PHS has struck out in directions with which, as professional scientists, we cannot in good conscience associate ourselves.

These directions are reflected in course offerings that fall into several categories. In the first category I place ordinary, harmless ideologies which are simply outside the reasonable purview of a humane society, such as courses in vegetarianism. In the second category, which is worse, are such egregious foolishnesses as psychic communication with pets, and planning vegetarian diets for carnivores. While they are potentially destructive — the latter of the health of pets and the former of the rational faculties of the students — these foolish activities present relatively small direct danger to pets and their owners. In the third category, which is positively pernicious, are courses advocating and promoting activism in what is called 'animal rights.' The point of view embodied in this ideology is very dangerous in that it threatens (and has already done measurable harm to) scientific and medical research of great importance to humans and to animals alike.

While we are not biological or medical scientists (rather, we are a research chemist and a professor of physics respectively) my wife and I must dissociate ourselves from these counterproductive activities. Because we still believe that PHS has important functions to carry out, we have withdrawn our support quietly and privately. But you have inquired as to the reasons behind our withdrawal, and I have therefore provided them. (I cannot resist the temptation to suggest that you and your staff have not yet trained your psychic powers well enough to have made this letter unnecessary.) We would, of course, be glad to hear from you further on these matters.

Sincerely yours,

Lawrence S. Lerner

# PENINSULA HUMANE SOCIETY

**12 AIRPORT BOULEVARD     SAN MATEO, CALIFORNIA   94401**
**(415) 573-3720**

July 23, 1988

Lawrence S. Lerner
10 Stadler Drive
Woodside, CA 94062

Dear Mr. Lerner:

I am in receipt of your letter of 12 July, 1988. I must confess that I am quite disappointed by the tone of your letter. For a man of science to suggest that there are certain areas of inquiry that are out of bounds says much about the state of modern science.

Rather than being the "objective quest for truth," science has seemingly devolved into a religious cult, complete with rigid orthodoxy and taboos. Actually, as we all know, science never was nor can be "objective." Heisenberg, for one, knocked that idea out of the ring. So to attack the efforts of the Peninsula Humane Society as it attempts to offer alternate points of view seems to me more like inquisitorial censorship than rational response.

Let me address some of your remarks. For openers, you characterize our course on vegetarianism as a harmless ideology. I think it rather intuitive of you to use the word harmless, for indeed a vegetarian diet does no harm, either to one's body or one's spirit. As to whether vegetarianism is an ideology, I think that may be a little strong. In any event, Peninsula Humane Society has, in one of its policy statements, come out in opposition to factory farming. Since non-factory-farmed animal products are rather difficult to come by, a reasonable alternative - from a number of points of view - is a vegetarian diet. So you see, vegetarianism is most definitely "within our purview."

As for the "foolishness" of psychic communication or vegetarian diets for pets, once again I must ask, why should these legitimate areas of inquiry be rendered taboo? What is it in them that you fear? There is ample evidence, gathered by your very own scientific community, to support the idea of forms of communication that transcend our usual definitions. I'm not talking "Twilight Zone" here; I'm speaking of rigorous scientific observation and testing. Simply because we cannot, yet, locate and measure the energy forms through which such transferences occur does not mean they don't happen any more than bacteria failed to exist before the microscope.

As for vegetarian diets for pets: if the planet truly cannot sustain an animal-based diet, and vegetarianism becomes of necessity the norm, either we must find a workable substitute for

*ADVOCATING QUALITY AND COMPASSION FOR ALL LIFE*

our pets - or we must cease having pets. Better we begin to explore these issues while we have time.

Last, we come to the "pernicious" courses on animal rights. Let me make two claims. One, there is an increasing body of evidence - gathered, I might add, by some of the most reputable scientific practitioners who have come to question the ethics of what they are doing - which demonstrates that the useful amount of knowledge gained through all the billions of dollars spent and millions of animals sacrificed is virtually trivial in comparison to the input. Two, any knowledge gained through cruelty and contempt is tainted knowledge and not worth having.

I think the recent controversy over the appropriateness of using scientific knowledge gained by the Nazis in their camps speaks most eloquently to the latter point. The dictates of a corrupt science not withstanding, the ends <u>never</u> justify the means. This statement has been echoed in every religion and major philosophical system. All life is sacred, and we cannot torture and murder innocent animals (and to deny that characterization of most animal-based biomedical research is to be ignorant) without doing grave damage to our collective humanity - which in the end is of much greater importance than simply pleasing this year's grant funding agency!

In Hindu religion, one way they talk of levels of spiritual growth is by reference to a metaphorical path along the spine, from the bottom up. Each stage is called a chakra. The third chakra is the urge to physical mastery and control. It is the last stage at which humans are still living essentially at their animal level. There is in science this same urge to master the physical universe - to achieve limitless energy, conquer time and space, even achieve immortality. A Faustian urge, no less.

The fourth chakra, however, is located at the heart. It is the chakra of compassion, and it is here that we begin to truly be human. You might argue that our compassion for our fellow humans makes us brutalize animals so as to find medical cures. The error in that line of reasoning is the idea that there is a fundamental difference between our fellow humans and other life forms. In truth we are all part of the same life force. To brutalize one to save the other is a zero sum game. Finally, to fail to recognize the inescapability of human suffering and the necessity of death is to completely miscomprehend the nature of this physical reality and the vehicles through which we learn and grow.

We are not, as I think you are inferring between the lines, a bunch of "kooks." Nor are we unaware of what we are about. Perhaps the problem lies in your definition of a humane society.

If you are thinking of us solely in terms of a holding pen, where some dogs and cats are adopted while the "excess" are destroyed, then you have a very limited, utilitarian view of our mission. We are not a mere commodities wholesaler, some kind of cut-rate pet store. Rather, we exists to set an example of compassion and humaneness, thereby diminishing those acts of cruelty and neglect the evidence of which we confront daily. In fact, when the humane movement began, over a hundred years ago, it was as much concerned with the plight of women and children as it was with animals.

We are, in effect, teachers. What we teach is an ethic through which humanity can rise above its own animal concerns and achieve a higher level of spiritual understanding regarding the meaning of compassion and the interrelatedness of all of life.

The world is in a rather serious state, and we are opening up certain lines of inquiry because we believe they may hold a key to the next stage in human evolution. Therefore, I am saddened to see people of science suggesting we turn back the clock and remain in a state of spiritual ignorance.

My rebuttal to your assertions has been necessarily superficial. To do them justice would take a book, at least. Nonetheless, I hope I have managed to convey to you the seriousness of our purpose.

Whether we are right or wrong, whether we succeed or fail, the important thing is to face the terror with open and honest hearts and minds.

I'm sorry, Mr. Lerner, that you cannot give fair hearing to these ideas. I think if you actually came and listened to some of our speakers you would find them to be quite sane, sensible, intelligent, honest, and intellectually stimulating. In fact, there are courses in our catalog that represent some of the most exciting discoveries and re-discoveries currently being explored by humanity. The stakes are not trivial, Mr. Lerner, and neither are we.

Sincerely,

*Ric Mállamo*

Ric Mállamo
Executive Director (acting)

RM:np

PENINSULA HUMANE SOCIETY

Many organizations have been taken over covertly over a period of time rather than through a recognizable overthrow. As mentioned earlier, The Humane Society of the United States is now a radical animal rights organization. Even the ASPCA, the oldest American animal welfare society, has switched positions. The ASPCA offers an animal rights handbook to its members and its direct-mail campaign shows a radical orientation. Time will tell how entrenched this position is, as it has a new president, Roger Caras, at the helm.

**Appropriating Independent Decisions**
Animal rights advocates appropriate animal rights issues that industries have nearly resolved, popularize the issue and then claim credit for forcing a desired result. This technique is convenient for raising funds throughout the course of the controversy.

For example, Avon, a national cosmetic company, became a target of a 1989 boycott by PETA for its use of animals for testing. The entire force of PETA's publicity machine came to bear on the company for four months, at which time Avon announced a policy of no more animal use. PETA claimed success; the giant had ostensibly been brought to its knees and converted to the animal rights point of view. After the victory celebration in the press, Avon produced statistics that showed that since 1981 it had been dramatically reducing the number of animals used in cosmetics testing. It had gone from using 14,550 animals in 1981 to using 2,243 animals in 1988. Additionally, in 1986, Avon had published a brochure declaring its intent to eliminate completely product-safety testing using animals. By 1989, it was on the verge of achieving its goal, but the public was not generally aware of either the program or its progress. Hence, it was ripe for media exploitation by animal rights advocates.

The same scenario exists in the dog and cat world, with animal rights forces using the practice of euthanasia as an emotional springboard to mount a campaign against an overpopulation problem that has been steadily on the road to resolution for more than 20 years. This situation has not been a matter of general public attention or knowledge, so the same tactics are possible. Animal rights forces are demanding action, claiming victories and raising funds from the publicity. Considering the number of pet owners and stray animals in this country, this offers a potentially endless supply of ammunition for propaganda and direct-mail solicitations.

This endless financial potential is related to another tactic: that of attacking practices that cannot be stopped or publicly whipping organizations for failing to use nonexistent enforcement authority. To explain this confusing situation, bear in mind that the American Kennel Club (AKC) is consistently targeted for censure by animal rights advocates for its failure to put puppy mills out of business. Puppy mills are commonly understood to be substandard commercial kennels that produce puppies without consideration for the health or well being of the animals used for propagation. The animal rights advocates, however, prefer to use the term to mean any kennel that produces numerous puppies for sale to the public or pet stores.

The AKC, however, is a registry; it has no enforcement authority in animal-abuse situations. It can, and does, refuse registry to animal abusers. State, county and city governments and the United States Department of Agriculture are the authorities that determine or sanction abuse. The AKC does not.

Another tactic used by animal rights advocates is describing current industries in terms representing obsolete methods and operations. The fur industry is constantly being denigrated in publications for inhumane, killing methods, such as rectal electrocution and neck breaking, when the industry has for years been using cool carbon monoxide gas. In fact, more than 90 percent of American fur farms voluntarily participate in independent veterinarian inspection and certification programs to guarantee humane care standards and guidelines for confinement, raising, breeding, and euthanasia of fur-bearing animals.

Lastly, a classic tactic is the use of staged media events. This ploy cuts across nearly all animal rights activities that make the news and which exploit, outrage or cater to the bizarre to attract attention. Instances of such conduct include promoting vegetarianism by buying a full-page ad in the *Des Moines Register* that equates meat-eating with serial killer Jeffrey Dahmer's cannibalism; using the celebration at the World Pork Expo to smash a cream pie in the face of 19-year-old Pork Queen Dainna Jellings; videotaping the euthanasia of dogs and cats and litters of kittens for evening news broadcasting to arouse public interest in legislation; producing movies that purport to show real animal hunters while actually using actors paid to slaughter on film.

This overview of promotional techniques and tactics used so effectively by the animal rights advocates demonstrates that the perception of man's relationship to animals has altered dramatically. It is time for the public to become aware of just what might happen if the animal rights advocates succeed in establishing their agenda. ⌗

# SECTION III

## Case Studies

# ⊞ CHAPTER 6. Sinking the Tuna Fleet

Steve Medina is a professional tuna fisherman who likes to talk to school children about commercial fishing. He enjoys the kids and interacts well with them. Unfortunately, he doesn't have the time to go to schools as much as he'd like because he's away from San Diego anywhere from 30 to 90 days at a time, three or four times a year, trying to catch tuna.

For Steve's family, tuna fishing has been their livelihood for four generations, and they can't imagine a more fulfilling form of earning a living. It's the kind of existence that offers them rewards in direct proportion to the amount of hard work and careful observation invested. Their experiences in the Eastern Tropical Pacific Ocean (ETPO) suggest to them that, with proper fishery management, tuna is a resource that could provide an endless supply of quality food in the form of yellowfin tuna. There is a special spirit and competition among those who fish this area. They're all after the same thing and are intent on preserving their way of life. The tuna boats from different countries are refereed, researched and monitored within the Eastern Tropical Pacific tuna fishery by the Inter-American Tropical Tuna Commission (IATTC). Since the 1950s, the IATTC has acted as an international buffer to preserve and enhance constructive fishing practices in this area. The commission serves as a vehicle for identifying and solving fishery problems and transferring positive trade practices from one country to another.

Before describing the current situation and how the animal rights movement has affected tuna commerce, a word about the basics of tuna fishing is necessary. How do you fish for tuna? First, you find them. Tuna school under logs or floating debris or certain species of dolphin. If you find one of these surface indicators, chances are that you will find tuna underneath. What's important to the fishermen is that the most mature members of the tastiest variety of tuna in the ETPO, the yellowfin, choose to school under dolphins in much greater numbers than under logs or debris. The three species of dolphins that associate with tuna (spotted, spinner and common dolphins) account for approximately nine and one half million of the total dolphin population in the Pacific Ocean. The remaining eight million dolphins of other species don't track with tuna at all. Hence, the ability to find a herd of the right kind of dolphin is invaluable to tuna fishermen.

This skill translates into larger fish per set of the nets. Larger fish, in turn, mean lower per-fish processing costs for the canneries. In this case, larger fish also mean that the less mature fish, which are in the prime reproductive stages of their lives, are not being caught and taken out of the stock replenishment cycle. If the fishermen can catch the bigger fish, it takes one-third to one-half as many tuna to fill a boat. This is considered beneficial because the alternative of taking smaller tuna would mean not only reducing the number of tuna of prime reproduction age, but also taking two to three times as many tuna per trip. Simple math suggests that harvesting immature yellowfin would ruin the fishery over time. A convenient peculiarity of the tuna schools under the dolphins is that they consist of primarily male tuna. No one has discovered where the females are, but educated guesses are that their life spans are shorter (perhaps three as opposed to five years for the males), or they are reproducing elsewhere. Regardless of the reason, taking the more mature males without a corresponding reduction in the female count would seem to enhance a stabilized fishery. The bottom line is that the mature yellowfin are more desirable from the standpoints of taste, processing costs and fishing efficiency.

After finding the tuna by sighting the dolphin, the most competitive and efficient method of capture involves the use of purse seine nets. The net is played out from the moving tuna boat, encircling the dolphins. It is weighted at the bottom and has floats at the top, so a curtain of net surrounds both the dolphin herd and the school of tuna. When the circle is complete, a line on the bottom of the net is pulled in like a drawstring, closing off the bottom escape route. The net is then retrieved. Over the years, the nets have been designed and improved to enhance the dolphins' ability to escape during capture. If they're not out by the time the net is ready to reel in, the boat moves backward in the water, lowering the far end of the net, enabling the dolphins to escape.

And, if that doesn't work, fishermen sometimes actually go into the nets to drive the dolphins out. There are cases of fishermen who have lost their lives trying to get dolphins out of the nets.

The object is to get the tuna close to the boat without dolphins in the nets. The dolphins are necessary for finding tuna, but then become a nuisance. Once the tuna nets are reeled up close to the boat, the fish are hauled into wells for storage, brining and freezing.

An average set of the net for a commercial tuna boat will bring in about 20 tons of fish. Setting on the right species of dolphin will bring in nearly all mature yellowfin, with very few other fish to sort out. A good voyage will bring back 800 to 1,000 tons of tuna. It sounds simple in principle, but it's a big ocean and there are innumerable possibilities for error. A boat, a crew, and IATTC approval are no guarantees of success, and even when good fortune does smile on boat and crew, they still know how hard they've worked for their rewards. The tuna industry has prospered for the last 40 years: the stocks have remained healthy; the fishermen of different countries have learned from each other; and, a valuable resource has been turned into a continual supply of high-quality, tasty, nutritious food. Distribution is world wide and the benefits are undeniable.

The problem is the perception that dolphins should not be harmed during the tuna harvest. This sentiment has caused an ongoing dispute in the tuna industry, but came to a head in the late 1980s. At that time, the animal rights movement was full-blown, pushing its publicity stunts and media shows on a number of fronts across the country.

One of the offerings in the propaganda show was an obscene film about fur seal hunting, which used staged animal mutilations. It purported to show the real-life scenes of seal hunting, but a later film by Icelandic film-maker Magnus Gudmundsson documented how animal activist fundraising films were staged. Gudmundsson was sued for libel in Oslo, but successfully defended himself when the court found that the activist film did, in fact, use such staging in their production.

Visual images in films generate an enormous amount of public sentiment because pictures stay in the memory much longer than a verbal account of the same thing. And when visual information happens to be based on half-truth or falsehood, dealing with this sentiment becomes an extremely difficult matter. Trying to refute an erroneous visual perception is almost impossible because the act of describing it (in order to refute it) actually reinforces it by bringing it to mind. Every time you bring it up, the visual image reasserts itself. False, dramatic, frightening, and horrible images are the worst to contend with for those who are trying to disseminate the true picture.

In the late 1980s, a movie was made about tuna fishing. An aging tuna boat, the *Maria Luisa,* was purchased at salvage rates, reconditioned but left outfitted with French nets (not the standard gear for the ETPO fleet), registered in Panama, manned by a Mexican crew and sent out into the Eastern Tropical Pacific. Tales about the relationship between the movie producer and the ship's captains (there were two of them) question who was running the show, but the crew is reported to have been frustrated and outraged by the conduct of at least one of the captains.

The reason for the controversy was shown in the movie; it amounted to a dolphin slaughter show. Nets were set in areas where the crew either knew or quickly discovered that there were no tuna underneath the dolphins, but they were drawn in anyway, capturing and entangling the dolphins and killing them. Not only were the French nets more deadly, but when the crew hauled the nets in, no one stopped to disentangle dolphins to keep them from being pulled through the reeling machinery. The power blocks, through which the dolphins were drawn, made mincemeat of them. The ship stayed out long enough to film the dolphin killing, but it never fished long enough to bring home a full load of tuna. The movie, in the view of ETPO tuna fishermen, was a repulsive hoax about tuna fishing and dolphin casualties in their waters. It was at first dismissed as being too obviously unbelievable to do any real damage. But, as the movie made its way through television and film audiences, viewers (who knew nothing about tuna fishing techniques) were outraged and horrified. It turned into a publicity bonanza for animal rights interests.

Tuna fishermen in the past had weathered disputes over dolphins being caught with the tuna. By 1990, however, they had underestimated the true strength, wealth and image-making power built up by the animal rights extremists. A combination of things were now in motion: the movie; a public over-sensitized by misinformation about animal welfare; increasing processor concerns about profit margins, market shares and public image; and the growing popularity of animal-rights issues. These combined factors produced an unexpected setback—Starkist went "dolphin safe." The definition of "dolphin-free tuna" means that the entire catch on any ship that killed a single dolphin in one of its sets is not considered dolphin free.

In April 1990, Starkist Tuna made an abrupt announcement that they would no longer process tuna that had been caught using techniques that killed dolphins at the same time. The news was a severe blow to the United States tuna fleet, primarily because the US tuna fleet had led the way in devising methods to reduce dolphin mortality while harvesting tuna.

Before Starkist's announcement, the ETPO had been fished by up to 124 United States tuna boats (1971). Today, seven remain, and those who continue the battle to harvest yellowfin in these waters wonder just how long you can fight over a principle. Most of the tuna boats that left are fishing in the Western Pacific, harvesting less desirable skipjack. The skipjack are not as tasty and they're smaller fish, but can be caught and sold with far less bother.

A look at statistics highlights the current risk of working in the ETPO. A normal set will bring in 20 tons of tuna. This means that about 40 to 50 sets take place on a normal voyage, and if a tuna boat goes out three or four times a year, that's 120 to 200 sets per boat per year.

Current statistics show that the US tuna boats in the ETPO take 400 to 500 dolphins per year with their tuna. This means that these seven tuna boats, on the worst average per-set basis possible are taking one dolphin in roughly every other set. Actual practice produces more zero-mortality sets, but the hazards of collapsing nets and unexpected sea conditions will claim a number of dolphins in a problem set. These mortality statistics are evidence of startling progress when one considers that the average dolphin herd is around 3,000 and the average number of dolphins encircled by nets is around 700. This means that one in about every 1,400 trapped dolphins (again, using the worst-case scenario) does not make it out of the nets. The trade-off is about 40 tons of tuna per single dolphin casualty.

From a wildlife management standpoint, these mortality rates have no effect on the sustainability of the dolphin population.

Game management studies show that up to 4 percent of a wildlife mammal population can be taken without affecting the stability of the stock. In this kind of projection, up to 400,000 dolphin could be lost without hurting their sustaining ability. In 1992, the total dolphin loss worldwide from all fishing for tuna by all countries is expected to come in at around 15,000. Statistically, they're safer from tuna boats than deer are from autos.

So Starkist, in avoiding the specter of market share loss through adverse publicity, or possibly a combination of other factors, initiated action that made it virtually impossible to sell yellowfin tuna in the United States. In addition, the Starkist business solution made it impossible for yellowfin to enter the country through purchases from processors outside the country. This situation occurred because activists sought and obtained a far-reaching court-imposed embargo to prevent the importing of improperly netted tuna from other countries or from brokers who do business with countries that allow dolphin sets. This ban has the entire industry tied up in knots and one of the world's largest consumers of tuna products is now off limits to yellowfin sales. A current battle also rages to reach resolution of the dilemma caused by the fact that the embargo has been determined to violate provisions of the General Agreement on Tariffs and Trade.

On top of this, legislation (HR5419) proposed by Rep. Gerry Studds (D-MA) and signed into law on October 26, 1992, could prohibit sets on marine mammals worldwide, effective March 1, 1994. Proposed penalties for violations include forfeiture of vessels and cargoes.

The legislative history goes back to the Marine Mammal Protection Act of 1972, amended in 1988. The current restrictions are a direct outgrowth of animal-rights advocates' pressure to adopt more severe federal regulations pertaining to the enforcement of the Act. The litigation front in this battle is strewn with tuna fishery casualties. Both administrative rulemakers and the legal community were pressured by animal rights interests toward using the letter of the original Act as a chokehold on the tuna industry. Tuna processors have been placed in the position of wielding the biggest club of all by rejecting entire boatloads of tuna.

The magnitude of this situation is not lost on federal officials who enforce administrative regulations in private industry, because the *big club* has never worked as an effective federal sanction against improper business practices. In this instance, however, animal rights forces have come up with a compelling arrangement, one the federal government had not been able to invent. It literally puts companies out of business through a combination of media, administrative rules, legal challenges, public opinion and market pressure. And it all goes back to years when courtroom concessions appeared small and bureaucratic specifications seemed distant. Today they appear, when weighed together, to be heavy enough to smother an entire segment of the tuna industry. The combination of embargo pressures, the passage of HR5419, public image problems and, ironically, the fleet's own success at lowering dolphin mortality rates has resulted in a situation in which it is impossible to run a tuna business. Considering the kind and number of turns in the industry that are now possible and unpredictable, animal rights activist Ronnie Lee's version of economic impossibility is a 1993 reality for smaller-scale tuna operators. And the rate of increasing complexity has the larger operators falling behind while planning business options.

The issue has been dolphin-centered all along (with no real concern expressed for the yellowfin), because the law and the situation provided the opportunity for control of an industry that was already interested in reducing dolphin mortality. To animal rights activists, the opportunities for fund raising, for gaining credibility and more legitimacy were irresistible. The effect has been to bring a portion of the tuna industry to its knees, worldwide. The industry includes not only fishermen and processors, but also distribution systems and suppliers. It's not simply a life and death issue for the dolphins, but rather an issue of absolute control by animal rights forces. The extremists won again, and without studies to show what might happen in a dolphin-enriched and under-fished yellowfin ocean, no one knows what the game management effect will be. Similarly, when Mexico decides to send its 50 boats to add to the 200 or so which have already moved to the Western Pacific to chase skipjack, no one knows what that kind of pressure will do to the skipjack fishery.

The tuna fishermen, over the course of this battle, have endured adverse publicity, legislative attacks, public scorn and regulatory harassment. They were not a politically aggressive group over this issue until it became apparent that every line of the Marine Mammal Protection Act would be used in every possible way against them. Representatives from nine countries have since formed a scientific advisory board to the Inter-American Tropical Tuna Commission and have signed an international resource management agreement. This agreement is based on their joint experience and is consistent with information produced by the National Academy of Sciences, National Research Council, in a report entitled "Dolphins and the Tuna Industry" (Commission on Life Sciences, 1990).

The tuna industry is still trying to figure out how to combat the producers and director of the *Maria Luisa* dolphin-slaughter film. But, in the meantime, the director is in Europe whipping up more storms of outrage by showing the film to unsuspecting audiences.

Although there is confidence that the ETPO can be managed in such a way as to provide a continuous tuna fishery without harm to dolphin stocks, there is still some question as to whether the industry will ever recover from the all-out assault by the animal rights movement. Steve Medina is still fishing, but not in the ETPO. He's further west, harvesting skipjack and looking over his shoulder. What could animal activists possibly find wrong with catching skipjack? ✛

# CHAPTER 7. The Raid on Dr. Taub's Laboratory

Getting a Job in a Lab *The most valuable research effort of all is to get a job in a lab (or any other facility that exploits animals). You should very seriously consider doing this if you are not yet known in your community as an animal rights activist...Here are some important points to remember...\*Don't give any hint that you are pro-animal rights or even vegetarian. \*If hired, don't go to animal-rights meetings or events. \*A 3 – 11 p.m. or overnight shift may offer more freedom to document abuses and gain information...\*If at all possible, take photographs and/or video tapes...\*If you do get a job, contact PETA's Research and Investigation Department for advice on how to proceed.*

From "Becoming an Activist: PETA'S Guide to Animal Rights Organizing," by Sue Brebner and Debbie Baer

Medical research using animals has been a target from the beginning of the animal welfare movement. Last century, when the humane societies were being formed, concern arose not only for animals used in bull-baiting, cat skinning and for those being worked to death, but also for those used in medical research. Only the obvious benefits of medical advances supported researchers. The extension of human life by 28 years since the turn of the century, cures for diseases and the elimination of pain for both humans and animals have been insurmountable arguments in favor of animal research.

Even so, the extremists in the animal rights movement launched a campaign against all animal research to initiate their unique world view. They used burglary, property destruction, theft, propaganda, misinformation, political lobbying and harassment to get their points across. Their points were: 1) that the use of innocent animals in research was immoral; 2) that we have nothing left to learn from such efforts; and, 3) that we have other ways to discover the same information (such as cell cultures, computer modelling and live human experimentation). Their first point remains within the scope of personal opinion, however, the second and third contentions are scientifically inaccurate and based on a premise that does not address the immediate alleviation of human suffering. While the mainstream animal welfare organizations focused on program development and humane education regarding animal treatment, this extremist faction often placed animal lives in jeopardy for the sake of publicity, and destroyed valuable research in the process.

The case that catapulted the animal rights movement to center stage in the U.S., was the carefully conceived and highly coordinated media and legal system assault on Dr. Edward Taub's Silver Spring, Maryland, research work. In May 1981, Alex Pacheco, a founder of the People for the Ethical Treatment of Animals, volunteered for laboratory work in Dr. Taub's facility. He worked there for five months before instigating a protracted legal system and publicity assault which was directed against Dr. Taub's animals and his laboratory practices; and which dramatically affected his career and his work. Materials generated in this publicity campaign are still used today as part of PETA's fundraising activities; i.e., a photograph captioned "This is vivisection," showing a monkey strapped into what appears to be a torture apparatus and other items used in a videotape purporting to document the incident.

This episode set the course for what has become a recognizable mode of operation, similar to that used by animal rights extremists in the Berosini case eight years later, where an individual was the target. Tactics included subversive infiltration; sabotage; surprise; sensational, emotionalized and misleading news coverage; fundraising and legal action. The extremists also faked visual images that left grotesque pictures in the minds of the viewers. The campaign included legitimization through the use of authority and celebrity figures. It promoted activism and popular support through demonstrations. Even before the raid on Dr. Taub's laboratory, individuals in the entire chain of command from the Maryland Attorney General's office down to the Montgomery County police force were lined up against him. Cleveland Amory, TV actress Gretchen Wyler and others supported the activist operation; and Capitol area reporters helped turn the search and seizure into a media event.

Dr. Taub was unaware of the animal rights community and their connections right in his own back yard. He gave Pacheco the volunteer position, unaware of his involvement as co-founder of PETA. One of his graduate students questioned Pacheco's true interest in science, but Dr. Taub recalls dismissing the query by responding, "What have we got to lose?" The answer turned out to be, among other things, eight years.

Taub didn't know that an attorney member of the Montgomery County Council was also serving as counsel for the Montgomery County Humane Society, or that the Montgomery County Humane Society was then led by Jean Goldenburgh, one of the nine original members of PETA. The MCHS attorney also happened to be the heir of the most politically powerful family in Montgomery County, Maryland politics over the past 100 years. He had called both the Montgomery County police chief and the state's attorney general in charge of prosecutions prior to the filing of the complaint and the issuance of the search and seizure order to alert them to a developing situation. Dr. Taub was unaware of the players and was not prepared for Pacheco's surreptitious activities. Dr. Taub relates:

> Late at night, when no one was in the laboratory, and with the aid of an outside accomplice and walkie-talkies to warn of the possible approach of a laboratory staff member, Alex Pacheco took photographs that purported to show unsanitary conditions at the laboratory. However, no visitor or staff member who was in the laboratory at the time saw any conditions resembling those in the photographs he took. Testimony was given under oath to this effect by seven individuals; in particular, Dr. A. G. Perry, a Department of Agriculture veterinarian who made an official unannounced inspection of the monkey colony in the middle of the period when Pacheco was there. Nobody ever saw the conditions that Pacheco photographed. This is court testimony. In my first trial, Pacheco admitted to staging two of his photographs.

Dr. Taub's laboratory staff included two animal caretakers, who had missed only one day between them in the 14 months they had worked at the facility prior to the search. While Dr. Taub was on vacation and within 15 days of the search, his animal caretakers missed a total of seven days of work.

Pacheco went through Dr. Taub's files, photocopied records,

took lab slides and brought observers along on his late-night prowls. Five of these observers executed affidavits and four testified in court. The four were animal rights activists Dr. Michael W. Fox and John McArdle (mentioned earlier in this book in connection with the Humane Society of the United States, although McArdle was not with HSUS at the time); Donald Barnes (president of the National Antivivisection Society); and Geza Taleki. Ronnie Hawkins, the fifth observer, was a member of a Florida antivivisection society.

Armed with affidavits and the advice and assistance of the MCHS attorney noted above, the Montgomery County police department, and the state's attorney general in charge of prosecutions, Pacheco filed a complaint. A *high-profile* search and seizure order was carried out the next day. As Dr. Taub put it:

> The next morning, the police raided my laboratory. They not only confiscated my monkeys, but they also tossed my files and everybody's desk drawers. They seized laboratory records of important experiments going back several years.
>
> The search and seizure in my laboratory was planned well in advance to have maximum media coverage. It was, in fact, a media circus. I think it is important to note that the press was there before the search began. This is illegal. It violated the secrecy of the search warrant. The two main parties to the search warrant who knew about the planned events beforehand were Alex Pacheco of PETA and Sergeant Swain of the Montgomery County Police Department. Some of the national media were there, as were virtually all of the local media—the local media in Washington, D.C., being, in effect, the hometown media of the members of Congress. There was a virtual mob of people. This can be arranged only with a great deal of prior effort.
>
> Organizing things outside the lab was the public relations officer of the Montgomery County Police. What was she doing there? How did she know the media would be there and that she would be needed? Are public relations officers usually present at the execution of search warrants?

Dr. Taub was charged with 119 misdemeanor counts revolving around inadequate veterinary care, inadequate care and infliction of pain and suffering. Seven counts attached to each of the 17 monkeys. One hundred thirteen counts were dismissed at the first trial. Because Dr. Taub is a Ph.D., and not a doctor of veterinary medicine, it was determined that he was guilty of failing to provide adequate veterinary care by an outside veterinarian for six of the monkeys. The decision was made notwithstanding the fact that no animals were found to be impaired by insufficient veterinarian visits and despite Dr. Taub's recognition as an expert in this field, along with his 25 years of experience in it. The six counts were appealed and a new trial was held on the six counts. He was finally exonerated of all charges, but the litigation and return to research took eight years of his life, produced a stream of threats, harassment and intimidation, interrupted his research, colored the perspective of the National Institutes of Health, and temporarily destroyed his reputation.

The impact of the publicity was devastating, and not just in personal terms. Dr. Taub had recently developed techniques for substantially improving movement in some stroke patients. His research involved deafferentation, which used surgery to abolish sensation from one or both forelimbs of the monkeys to enable testing methods for rehabilitation of movement. It resulted in the development of new rehabilitation approaches for stroke victims and the development of thermal feedback, used to treat migraine, Reynaud's disease, hypertension and other disabling and painful stress-related conditions. With regard to the ultimate victims of the legal action, Taub explains:

> I had just been about to start applying my findings with deafferented monkeys to human stroke victims back in Silver Spring when my work was stopped for six years by PETA's actions. The start up of my research at the University of Alabama at Birmingham, where all practical arrangements had to be made anew, required another two years. Based on our preliminary research, I estimate that the new treatment is potentially applicable to approximately 50,000 people in the United States each year. The delay in getting the work done has been eight years. Thus, the actions of the antivivisectionists have

resulted in withholding the potential benefits of this treatment to a large number of impaired humans whose quality of life has been greatly compromised by their stroke. The term "humane," which is commonly used to refer to animal welfare societies, obviously cannot be said to apply to animal rights groups like PETA.

This account does not go into detail about the raging legal battles PETA conducted to obtain possession of, or prevent experimentation on, the 17 confiscated monkeys, and to prevent their euthanasia. PETA wanted to keep the monkeys alive even though experts, including one of their own appointed veterinarians, recommended euthanasia. The monkeys became pawns in a power game that had little to do with their well-being or quality of life. PETA, the Physicians' Committee for Responsible Medicine and the International Primate Protection League have all taken court action within the past 11 years to prevent euthanasia and/or experimentation on the deafferented monkeys. The rub for the activists was that euthanasia would permit experimentation prior to death under anesthesia and that occurrence, especially as the monkeys got older, could be of value to medical research. They didn't want research expectations to be validated in any way, and they especially did not want it confirmed through more experimentation. PETA's actions were directed toward having the monkeys die without further experimentation, as one did painfully in August 1989, while PETA held a restraining order against euthanasia. Subsequent tests after NIH court action (and after at least two blue-ribbon panels had recommended euthanasia for specific deafferented monkeys) proved to be encouraging for rehabilitation efforts for brain and spinal cord injury victims.

After the confiscation, the monkeys stayed in an NIH facility in Poolesville, Maryland, for five years. Two of the 17 monkeys died during this stay from non-research related causes. In 1986, five of the six control monkeys went to the San Diego Zoo. The remaining nine experimental monkeys and one control monkey went to the Delta Primate Center in Covington, Louisiana. Today, one experimental monkey and the control monkey remain at the Louisiana Center.

The monkeys are still being exploited by activists to further the goals of the animal rights movement. Dr. Taub reported that they produced a 15-minute video in 1981, which focuses on the Silver Spring monkeys and purports to tell the story of Dr. Taub's laboratory. The video uses pictures ostensibly taken by Pacheco during his volunteer work, but also uses slides and photos from Dr. Taub's files, some of which were 10 to 20 years old in 1981. The misleading photos are disturbing, but what is worse, according to Taub, is that "fifty-two specific comments on the voice-over narration of the video are wrong and there are 73 identifiable errors in the video—all in a 15-minute video." Dr. Taub's contacts with the press are usually prefaced by his query as to whether they have seen the video. If they have, he asks them to watch it again and talk about it before moving to the questions they had in mind. It changes the entire tone of the interviews.

Dr. Taub knows that he could sue the video's producers, but he reflects on the loss of eight years of his research work and the delay in advances to improve the lives of stroke victims and confesses, "I have a life to live and a research career to pursue. If I sued, I would spend all my time in court. I know—I've done that before." He also observes that even if he sued and won, he would be doing what the animal rights extremists want him to do, which is to provide them with more publicity and to stop his research. He has personally resolved his dilemma in favor of producing research results. "It's too bad. The public really needs to know what's going on," he adds.

Dr. Taub is joined in his feelings by the president of U.S. Surgical, who was targeted for murder by an animal activist; by Dr. John Orem, of Texas Tech University who lost at least a year of research on sudden infant death syndrome and $50,000 worth of equipment; by Dr. Adrian Morrison, a fellow researcher who supported Dr. Taub and who—as a result of his support—had his own lab broken into in 1990. Morrison, following the break-in, found himself characterized in the media as an "animal Nazi." Later, an article appeared in the *Village Voice* newspaper which relied on material stolen from his lab files. Copies of the article were mailed to his neighbors with a letter citing Morrison's home address. While in Italy, he was further harassed by animal rights picketers who had been alerted to his whereabouts. Toxicology expert Dr. Richard Aulerich of Michigan State University also knows the sting of animal liberation, having lost 32 years of research data through an animal rights arson attack on his office and an MSU mink research facility in early 1992 ($125,000 damage). Some of the many other researchers and universities that have been attacked are noted in chapter 9.

These people carry on with their work, but now wear the stressed expression of people who have been hurt or violated—the same expressions worn by victims of muggings, returning hostages and others who have lived through disastrous circumstances. Further, they are keenly aware that their professional lives can be wrenched from them without warning—through media attacks, legal system maneuvering, added regulations, character assassination. The list of animal activist/terrorist weapons is extensive enough to make defense preparations impossible: medical researchers can't become lawyers, public image experts, lobbyists, home security specialists or regulatory experts without virtually ending their research careers.

Researchers don't feel that they have huge amounts of time to lose. Depending on their specific pursuit, they are aware that lost time translates into prolonged pain, debilitation and premature death. They're also aware that time is not the only enemy. The cost of a laboratory cat has gone from $30 to $200 within the past five years; studies in certain areas, such as addictions, have declined by 50% over the same period, and fewer bright young students are choosing careers in life sciences.

These scientists have shared the hope that the nightmare will go away, and view their lifetimes of preparation and current research as races for human progress and against death and debilitation. With the normal needs for family lives and community, along with demanding careers, there is no free time: defending themselves or their work exacts a daily toll in human suffering in terms of delayed or denied research findings. These people can't afford to stop their work to fight about the need for its existence; they feel vulnerable to being set up; they need affirmation of their work from outside the scientific community; and they ache for public awareness of the magnitude and full effect of animal activist terrorism. ⊕

# CHAPTER 8. The Las Vegas Affair

Bobby Berosini was not the first person to be attacked in public by animal rights propaganda, but he was the first to fight back successfully. He had two advantages over others who had been on the animal rights torture rack since the mid '80s: He had no fellow professionals or parent institution to tell him to be quiet, take the hits, and hope that his attackers would go away. As a Las Vegas animal trainer and entertainer for the Stardust Hotel, he was a lone target, and knew that his livelihood was at stake from the instant the publicity hit the local television news.

His second advantage was having grown up in Czechoslovakia during a time when all one's possessions and property could be taken away by someone else's version of "what's best for the people." In fact, his father, an animal trainer and circus owner, had his castle and land taken from him when communism arrived. In comparing that portion of his life with his current harassment by the animal rightists, Berosini observes: "In Czechoslovakia, when they came in the name of the people and took everything we had it was bad enough, but this time when they came in the name of the animals it was too damn much." He had seen it all before and would not give up again without a fight.

On August 2, 1989, Bobby Berosini, Ltd. filed a suit for invasion of privacy and defamation against PETA in the Clark County, Nevada District County, Nevada District Court. The basis of the lawsuit was that PETA, 1) falsely accused Berosini of abusing his orangutans and, 2) distributed an altered videotape that supposedly proved this abuse.

The lawsuit claimed that:

- in the spring of 1989, PETA began a formal, multi-million dollar fundraising campaign based on stopping the use of animals in entertainment;
- PETA identified Berosini as a principal target in the fundraising campaign;

- PETA contacted entertainers employed in the act in which Berosini's orangutans appeared;
- at PETA's urging, some of these entertainers intentionally taunted and incited the orangutans, creating a situation in which the animals could become violent and which required Berosini to control the animals to prevent them from hurting themselves or the audience. An entertainer working with PETA secretly filmed Berosini trying to get the animals under control;
- PETA edited and altered the tapes and then distributed the doctored tapes; and
- PETA commenced to wage a massive misinformation media campaign falsely accusing Berosini of criminal abuse, falsely calling him a child abuser, falsely stating that he beat the orangutans with a steel pipe, and falsely stating that the striking of the orangutans was routine and unprovoked.

Based on PETA's misrepresentations, the U. S. Department of Agriculture, Animal and Plant Health Inspection Service (APHIS) conducted an in-depth investigation, including an on-site inspection of the facilities and the orangutans. APHIS issued an official announcement that it had found no signs of abuse.

Similarly, pursuant to a court order, two world-renowned experts, Dr. Richard Simmonds, DVM, MS, and Dr. Kenneth G. Gould, Ph.D., B Vet Med, MRCVS, issued reports that the orangutans were in excellent health and had not been abused in any manner.

PETA then employed three experts to examine the orangutans. None of these experts would sign a report indicating abuse. In fact, PETA was fined by the court for trying to legitimize the report by filing and making public the unsigned and unsubstantiated report. It was never admitted into evidence.

PETA filed a counterclaim against Berosini requesting confiscation of the orangutans due to Berosini's alleged abuse. The court dismissed the counterclaim. PETA's lawyers were sanctioned by the trial court and reported to bar counsel for a number of reasons, including manufacturing evidence. The producer of the tape had admitted he altered the videotape to sensationalize it.

PETA was supported in its court action by two *amicus curiae* briefs. One of the briefs was jointly signed by the following organizations:

- Physicians Committee for Responsible Medicine
- Animal Welfare Institute
- Psychologists for the Ethical Treatment of Animals
- Humane Society of the United States (HSUS)
- American Society for the Prevention of Cruelty to Animals
- Fund for Animals
- International Primate Protection League
- Animal Legislative Defense Fund
- Association of Veterinarians for Animal Rights
- International Fund for Animal Welfare

After 29 days of hearing evidence, the jury found PETA guilty of defamation and invasion of privacy, and the court awarded Berosini damages. The defamation count required the jury to find that PETA knowingly, willingly and maliciously made false statements regarding Berosini's alleged abuse of the orangutans.

Although the jury had found PETA guilty, the organization continued its propaganda war against Berosini by issuing statements that:

- Berosini was caught on videotape beating the orangutans;
- Berosini routinely abuses his orangutans;
- the verdict by the jury was the result of bias, since the judge was a college roommate and former law partner of the owner of the Stardust Hotel;
- the jury found no malice on the part of PETA;
- the United States government, through the Departments of Interior and Agriculture, and the Berosinis were guilty of collusion;
- the Berosini case was one of "intimidation to silence all animal rights groups."

The above contains hints of common practices employed by animal rights organizations that the public seldom reads about and the press almost never reports. For instance:

- *Claims that seek confiscation of the animals.* Berosini's uninterrupted possession of his animals, although hotly contested by PETA, left no doubt as to their condition and treatment.
- *Infiltration.* The Berosini production company was infiltrated by animal rights activists who worked as regulars until conditions were right for the publicity campaign.
- *Media set-up.* The news media were used for a surprise attack against Berosini. When first confronted by the press, he had no idea of what had occurred and had no inkling that the media representatives had already been handed a full account of his alleged animal abuse.
- *Doctored evidence.* PETA submitted a doctored videotape to support its claim of abuse.

Bobby Berosini is a ninth-generation animal trainer. His entire life has been devoted to his animals, who are as much a part of the family as children, and require so much attention that it's nearly impossible to leave them for even short vacations. Berosini and his wife, Joan, live and work in Las Vegas, Nevada. Their act features Berosini and his orangutans, singers, dancers, skaters, music and a light show.

On the night the news reporter and Berosini's attorney showed up, friends called the Berosinis to tell them that television stations were airing a story about Berosini abusing his orangutans, and it looked very bad. "As if on cue, our phone started ringing off the hook," recalls Joan, "with death threats, abuse and vile language hurled at us."

Concerned about their scheduled performances, they called the general manager of the Stardust Hotel who told them to go on with the show. However, a hotel clerk called Berosini and begged him not to come in because she feared for their lives. There were 200 pickets at the Stardust. "Our billboards with Bobby's picture were being defaced, while the TV cameras rolled. The phone was ringing incessantly and threatening...I canceled our shows," Joan recalls.

The shock from the media blitz and the horrible publicity for everyone attached to the show drove Bobby to bed dazed that night. Joan remembers that night vividly: "Bobby went to bed and pulled the covers over his head. He said he wanted to die. We were scrambling...We had devoted our lives to our work and our animals. Our whole life turned around the needs of the animals. We were in shock. I had worked with Bobby and the animals for over 20 years...I have never been surrounded with so much hate in all of my life."

A bright moment occurred when counter-picketing began in Berosini's favor. The Berosinis decided to fight back and sought counsel on what they could do. Bobby and Joan granted the press interviews and invited anyone to inspect the animals for signs of abuse, challenging that if it could be shown, he would donate the animals to any organization anywhere in the world. Leaders of two of the local animal groups accepted the challenge, but found no such signs and promptly called off their people who were picketing. Strangely, PETA did not accept that invitation to inspect the animals. Joan remembers Jeanne Roush telling the press that she "wouldn't waste her time."

It's not surprising that Jeanne Roush (who has recently replaced Kim Stallwood as executive director of PETA) didn't waste time on the possibility of generating favorable publicity for the Berosinis. Once PETA had obtained its videotape evidence, the condition of the animals lost importance, although PETA leaders may have wanted them out of the entertainment business. Animal rights organizations, like PETA, have consistently claimed and demonstrated that animals are better off dead than enslaved and confined by human beings. In fact, Ingrid Newkirk has observed that euthanasia beats the socks off the option of rabbits being stuck in a hutch and bred. PETA's idea of abuse includes simply having animals as pets. This belief, widely articulated by animal rights extremists, means that if Berosini does not act merely as a benevolent guardian for his animals, regardless of how well he may care for them as entertainers, they would be better off dead than living under such conditions.

On August 2, 1989, five days after the story broke, the Berosinis filed their lawsuit charging defamation, invasion of privacy, misappropriation of name and likeness (fundraising using the Berosini name), conspiracy and business interference. PETA then filed its countersuit, which was subsequently dismissed. Investigations by the U. S. Departments of Agriculture (USDA) and the Interior (USDI) found no evidence to support PETA's claims. Unfortunately, however, during the pendency of the trial the USDI suspended Berosini's license to buy, sell or transport endangered species across state lines. It took him more than $250,000 and until June 1992 to complete the process of reinstating his license.

Bobby Berosini returned to perform at the Stardust Hotel and Casino on Wednesday, August 9, 1989, but because of continued threats, the Berosinis agreed to place their primates under a protective watch by the Humane Society of Southern Nevada and the Society for the Prevention of Cruelty to Animals. This protective custody agreement lasted until representatives from these animal welfare organizations felt it was appropriate to discontinue safety precautions and security coverage. Representatives were present during each of the performances for months. Part of the protective custody agreement read: "We have further decided that it would be in the best interest of the primates that they remain in the possession of the Berosinis. We personally feel that it would be an unacceptable endangerment and potentially life-threatening to the orangutans and the chimpanzee to attempt to move them to any other facility. The social and psychological interaction between Mr. Bobby Berosini and his primates, as well as the primates' physical dependence upon Mr. Berosini unequivocally mandates that he is the most qualified person to look after them."

The animal welfare organizations investigated charges by PETA, examined the premises, each animal and the performance practices of Berosini, assessed the qualifications and experience of his animal handlers, and concluded:

> After a thorough physical analysis and scientific investigation, it is the conclusion of the Humane Society of Southern Nevada & SPCA that there exists no foundation to justify or warrant abuse, cruelty or neglect charges against Bobby Berosini, his handlers nor any member of the Berosini family. The physical evidence does not support the videotape nor allegations by representatives of PETA that Bobby Berosini, Sr. repeatedly struck his animals with steel bars wrapped in electrical tape. All of the animals in the possession of Bobby Berosini, LTD are in excellent condition.

On August 11, 1990, a jury awarded Berosini $4.7 million in damages. The judge ruled on the jury's determination and interpreted their findings as warranting an award of $3.1 million, plus legal fees and court costs. The case was still in the appeal process in late 1992, and Berosini will probably continue to be an item in *PETA News*.

The court action has not ended the ordeal. Even after the judgment, the harassment continued with threats involving death, bombs, and theft of the animals. Berosini's attorney also became involved in the vilification, receiving threats and dead birds in the mail.

Lest the Berosini case appear to stand as an isolated instance, other animal-user lives and livelihoods have been ruined or scarred forever by the extremists in the animal rights movement. The similarities of what happened to Dr. Edward Taub (see Ch. 7) and Bobby Berosini are striking. The Taub case started in 1981, and although his personal involvement in the court actions are over, animal rights legal maneuverings continue in that case to this day. It will be interesting to see whether PETA's reaction to the Berosini appeal will follow the format established when Dr. Taub was finally exonerated of all charges in court. At that time, the matter was at the state supreme court level and the decision turned on an issue that finally resolved the case (three possibilities existed for deciding the case in Taub's favor, but two would have allowed continued appeals). When the decision was issued, animal rights groups used the defeat to claim that Dr. Taub had escaped on a technicality. Fundraising naturally followed the issuance of the decision. In similar fashion, regardless of the Berosini outcome, animal rights groups will be poised to claim a renewed reason for fundraising.

The next chapter provides a sampling of publicized activities from 1983 to 1992. ✠

# ⊞ CHAPTER 9. Raids and Destruction

The information presented in this chapter covers the years 1984 to 1989, and includes incidents that occurred in the United States, England and Europe. The following incidents are presented to demonstrate the intensity of animal rights extremists and the lengths to which they'll go to gain publicity for their cause. The items that follow provide the backdrop for the attack against the Berosinis and originate from the court records of their trial (*Bohumil Berousek aka Bobby Berosini vs. People for the Ethical Treatment of Animals, et al.*, case number A276505, District Court, Clark County, Nevada, decided September 11, 1990). These items represent only a small portion of the extensive number of raids and acts of violence that have occurred in the past decade and continue to occur. They prove that the animal rights extremists are to be taken seriously.

■    An antivivisectionist group placed a bomb in the yard of a Chicago researcher's home in early 1982. The bomb burned out before triggering an explosion that "would certainly have killed the family dog." The story did not identify the group or print the exact date of the attempted bombing. (*Chicago Tribune*, "Foes of Animal Research Baring Teeth in Protest," March 20, 1983.

■    Band of Mercy members stole 40 rabbits from a laboratory at the University of Maryland. (April 1982)

■    A letter bomb, sent to the office of former British Prime Minister Margaret Thatcher, scorched the face and hair of an office manager. Three similar incendiary letter bombs were sent on the same day to several members of the British Parliament, but were detected before they exploded. The Animal Rights Militia claimed responsibility. (November 30, 1982)

■ The Animal Liberation Front broke into the Howard University Medical School and stole 28 cats, many of which were involved in studies on nerve transmission. Property damage and loss of animals were estimated at $2,640. ( December 25, 1982)

■ The Animal Liberation Front freed two rats from their cages at the University of Florida School of Medicine. (December 25, 1982)

■ The Animal Liberation Front entered the United States Naval Medical Research Institute and stole a dog involved in hyperbaric chamber research studies. (December 28, 1982.)

■ A group calling itself the Urban Gorillas stole three cats from a psychology laboratory at the University of California, Berkeley. The animals were being used in studies to determine how visual images are processed in the brain. (December 28, 1982)

■ Researchers at the University of British Columbia were subjected to threatening telephone calls, hate mail and had antivivisectionist slogans spray-painted on their homes. One protester threatened to break the kneecaps of the university coordinator of the Animal Care Center. (1982)

■ The Animal Liberation Front stole several dogs from the United States Naval Medical Research Institute. (January 14, 1983)

■ The campus police of the University of California, Davis observed a young woman climbing over the fence to the primate research center. Police immediately searched the area but could not locate the intruder. A cage was found unlocked, but no animals were missing. (January 20, 1983)

■ Animal rights militants sent letter bombs to Britain's agricultural minister, Canada's diplomatic mission, the University of Bristol's Veterinary School in Weston-Super-Hare in Western England, and a scientist's home in Cambridge. (February 5, 1983)

■ Life Force Foundation members made an unannounced inspection of a laboratory at the University of California, San

Francisco and harassed the scientist. His research, on the neural control of eye movement, is conducted with monkeys, whose visual system is similar to humans. (July 1983)

■ The Animal Liberation Front stole 12 dogs, including five with experimental pacemakers, from the Harbor University of California, Los Angeles Medical Center in Torrance, California. The animals were used in heart research. (December 25, 1983)

■ The Animal Liberation Front took six rats used in research on Alzheimer's disease from Johns Hopkins University. In a prepared statement, ALF stated that the animals were "fellow travelers on this planet" and should not be used for "painful, pointless, and repulsive" experiments. (December 25, 1983)

■ British animal rights activists staged a protest at Hazelton Laboratories in Harrogate, England. Approximately 700 to 800 people took part in the demonstration that resulted in a clash with local police when protesters attempted to break through the laboratories' security fence. (January 28, 1984)

■ Approximately 500 police officers were needed during an animal rights protest at a mink-breeding farm near Warwickshire, England. Ironically, police horses were injured when the officers tried to contain the 2,000 demonstrators. Protesters released some of the mink, who escaped into the woods. Some were later found dead, presumably because they were unable to survive on their own. (January 29, 1984)

■ Mobilization for Animals demonstrators blocked the driveway of the California Primate Research Center and prevented employees from entering the facility at the University of California, Davis. Police arrested 15 protesters. (April 24, 1984)

■ The Animal Liberation Front broke into a psychology laboratory at California State University, Sacramento and stole 20 rats. The research, on positive reinforcement of behavior, had potential application to the treatment of autism. (May 16, 1984)

■ A University of Pennsylvania medical laboratory was

broken into and vandalized by Animal Liberation Front members, who also stole video and audio tapes documenting six years worth of primate research designed to improve the prevention, diagnosis and treatment of head injuries. ALF also poured chemicals into the computers and damaged other equipment. (May 28, 1984)

■ The Animal Liberation Front broke into the University of Pennsylvania Veterinary School and stole dogs being used in arthritis research, cats being studied to determine the neurological basis of sudden infant death syndrome, and pigeons being used in wing-repair research. (July 28, 1984)

■ Twenty-six demonstrators were arrested when they blocked the main entrance to the system-wide administration offices of the University of California, Berkeley. The Animal Rights Direct Coalition, based in Sacramento, California, was demanding personnel changes in the Psychology Department and the Berkeley Animal Care Committee. (August 27, 1984)

■ In England, the Animal Liberation Front turned to product tampering to publicize the use of animals used for testing. Bottles of shampoo contaminated with bleach were found in drug stores in London, Leeds and Southhampton after ALF issued a warning that the shampoo might be dangerous.

■ According to the Associated Press, animal rights extremists freed 2,000 minks from a fur farm in northern England. The Royal Society for the Prevention of Cruelty to Animals condemned the action as "downright bloody stupid... [It] will cause suffering to wildlife in the area as well as the mink themselves," said a spokesperson for the organization. "It is doubtful anyway whether that number of mink could survive in these conditions, " he added. Employees of the fur farm, aided by police and fire officials, captured most of the mink. (November 4, 1984)

■ A Columbus, Ohio, animal rights activist was arrested for trespassing while protesting research using cats at a Ohio State University dentistry lab. The project involved electrical stimulation to bone, which could be useful in increasing the rate of orthodontic tooth movement. (November 17, 1984)

■ To protest the use of monkeys in tooth decay research, the Animal Liberation Front in England announced that its members had injected rat poison into selected Mars Bars chocolate candy already on store shelves. The manufacturer of the candy removed the candy bars from stores. (November 18, 1984)

■ The National Cancer Institute was notified that an Allentown, Pennsylvania, newspaper received a letter from the Animal Liberation Front stating that an institute would be bombed to protest Dr. Robert Weinberg's cancer research at the Whitehead Institute in Cambridge, Massachusetts. Dr. Weinberg also received threatening letters signed by ALF. The letters protested Weinberg's use of laboratory animals. A recent issue of *Science* reported that he uses tissue cultures, not live animals for experiments. (November 28, 1984)

■ Bomb threats were made against the University of Nevada School of Medicine as a protest against animal research. (November 30, 1984)

■ More than 100 laboratory animals were stolen from the City of Hope National Medical Center. The stolen animals included 36 dogs involved in cancer research, 11 cats used in neuromuscular studies, and 12 rabbits with oral monkey herpes. Animal Liberation Front claimed responsibility for the theft in a statement issued by an officer of the People for the Ethical Treatment of Animals. (December 9, 1984)

■ According to a *Baltimore Sun* newspaper article titled, "British fight for animal rights turns violent," the South East Animal Liberation League in England broke into the home of a scientist, David Walker, and attacked him with a fire extinguisher and stole files from his study. The Scottish Antivivisectionist Society published the home address of two scientists studying brain damage through research with animals and asked members to write letters of warning to the researchers. The scientists are under police protection. Also, the Hunt Saboteurs Association is campaigning against fishing, which a spokesman for the group described as "quite possibly one of the cruelest blood sports." Participants in a fishing contest were pelted with rocks from a van.

An offshoot group, Hunt Retribution Squad, spread broken glass on a soccer field because the manager of one of the soccer teams had advocated hunting in an interview. (December 16, 1984)

■ Animal Liberation Front members broke into the University of Western Ontario and stole three cats and one adult rhesus monkey. The monkey may be infected with herpes virus B, an infection that has been fatal in almost all humans who have developed symptoms. In response to the university's warning that the monkey was infected, ALF announced that it would kill the animal rather than return it to the university. (December 31, 1984)

■ The Animal Liberation Front claimed responsibility for placing two gasoline bombs outside the London home of Nobel Laureate Sir John Vane, director of research and development at the Wellcome Foundation. The fire was extinguished before it spread beyond the garage. A second bomb was thrown at the residence of another Wellcome administrator and four employees had missiles launched through their windows and their properties covered with paint. (January 7, 1985)

■ Five animal rights activists were found guilty of misdemeanor criminal trespassing in connection with an October 1984 demonstration at the Arizona Health Sciences Center. Three activists were sentenced to eight hours of community service, which included, for one defendant, the research and preparation of a report on the human health contributions of animal research. (February 1985)

■ Fred and Jan Hodgins, owners of a kennel that supplies animals to biomedical research, were awarded $329,739 in damages by a Wayne County, Michigan Circuit Court jury, that decided the couple had been defamed by animal rights activists.

■ Animal Liberation Front members left a threatening note and splattered red paint on the home and car of a Los Angeles County animal control officer as a protest against the sale of unclaimed pound animals to research laboratories. According to United Press International, the officer had received threatening calls from ALF. (March 11, 1985)

■ According to *The Atlanta Journal and Constitution*, burglars released three rhesus monkeys from a lab at Auburn University. Two of the monkeys returned on their own. One was captured by university security. (March 24, 1985)

■ At the University of California Veterinary School in Davis, 15 to 20 members of the People for the Ethical Treatment of Animals invaded a physiology laboratory in which surgery was being conducted on an anesthetized dog. The invaders objected to the use of the dog and disrupted the class, but no arrests were made. On June 9, 1985, warrants for trespassing were issued against seven of the invaders.

■ Seven members of the group, California for Responsible Research, were arrested and charged with disturbing the peace at the University of San Francisco Medical Center. Placard-carrying demonstrators attempted to block the entrance to a meeting of the Board of Regents. In an interview with local press, the group's leader said that even if his two-year-old daughter were sick, he would not condone research on animals to seek a cure for her illness. (1985)

■ For three weeks in July 1985, animal rights activists attempted to block gateways to laboratories at the New York State Psychiatric Institute. Demonstrators from the group, Human/Animal Liberation Front were protesting Parkinson's disease studies on primates. (1985)

■ In Ireland, members of the Animal Liberation Front told the news media that they had laced bottles of shampoo with bleach in three cities to protest the manufacturer's use of animals for cosmetic research. Bottles of the shampoo were removed from shelves in Dublin, Limerick and Kilkenny. (1985)

■ In Great Britain, 13 animal rights activists were tried and found guilty for what had been described as one of the most violent and well-organized assaults on a research institution in Europe. The convicted individuals had participated in an April 1985 raid on the Imperial Chemical Industries' Alderly Park site. The raid was conducted by 300 masked Animal Liberation Front members who, armed with crowbars, smashed windows and doors to break into several buildings. Animals and reports were stolen and more than $15,000 in damages were done to the facilities. (June 7, 1985)

■ Members of Last Chance for Animals, a California-based animal rights groups (formerly, 2nd Chance for Animals) climbed to the roof of one of the Cedars Sinai Hospital animal facilities and chained themselves to the railing. After being escorted from the building by local police, the group commandeered a van that is used to transport animals to the hospital from the San Bernardino, California, pound. This time the demonstrators chained themselves to the van. They were removed by police. The next month, the activists invaded the Los Angeles City Council chambers, demanding a stop to the sale of pound animals for research. Later, the demonstrators returned to the Cedars facility, climbed atop a canopy at the hospital entrance and chained themselves to the building. They were arrested and charged with trespassing. (September, October, and November, 1985)

■ Seven animal rights activists were convicted for blocking the entrance to the California Primate Research Center at the University of California, Davis. Municipal Court Judge Larry Frumes sentenced four of the defendants to five days of community service and one year probation. The other two demonstrators were sentenced to five days of community service and five days in jail. This was the first jury trial of animal rights activists in the country. The convicted activists were affiliated with Trans-Species Unlimited and another California-based group, Animal Rights Direct Action Coalition. (1985)

■ The Animal Liberation Front vandalized 11 Jaguar automobiles owned by a car-rental company in Thames Ditton, Surrey, England. The motive for the attack, according to investigators, was ALF's discovery that the company had been renting cars to police officers for following animal activists in London. (1985)

■ During 1985-86, the following petition was circulated by animal rights advocates in public places in California:

"I, the undersigned, feel it is unethical to use animals in medical scientific investigations. I, therefore, pledge to oppose all animal experimentation in medical research and further pledge that if I should become ill I will not receive any medicines, antibiotics, vaccines, diagnostic tests, treatments, or operations in which animal experimentation played a role in the development."

■ In telephone calls to newspapers, the Animal Rights Militia claimed responsibility for planting explosive devices outside the homes of four people involved in animal research in Great Britain. The devices were detonated in controlled explosions by army bomb disposal teams. A Home Office minister said that the bomb planting was "being treated as a serious crime, and will be vigorously investigated." The first bomb, a plastic container containing three butane gas cylinders, a battery and a clock, was found under a car belonging to the sales director of Shamrock Farms, a West Sussex firm that imports monkeys and breeds them for sale to research laboratories. The second bomb was discovered in London under the car of Dr. Brian Meldrum, who had headed an Institute of Psychiatry research team using baboons for studies on epilepsy. The third bomb was found on the front porch of the Harrogate home of Dr. Alan Armitage, scientific director of the Hazelton Research Laboratories. The fourth bomb was discovered on the doorstep of Professor Ted Evans, head of neuroscience at the University of Keele, Staffordshire. A Staffordshire police officer reported: "It was certainly an anti-personnel device and if any innocent person had been near the house this morning and the thing had gone off, then at the very least they would have sustained serious injuries." Ms. Diana Jones, Royal Society for the Prevention of Cruelty to Animals, said that her organization "regards this sort of action, as will all sane and sensible people, as an utter abomination." Ms. Emma Fox, Animal Liberation Front, said: "A lot of ALF members would totally agree with these tactics. I wouldn't be at all concerned if a vivisector was killed, compared with the death and suffering they cause to millions of animals." (January 8, 1986)

■ The Animal Liberation Front claimed responsibility for a break-in at the University of Toronto's dentistry building which caused more than $7,000 in damages, according to the *Chronicle of Higher Education*. ALF stated in a press release that the break-in was part of its "economic sabotage campaign against the scums who torture animals." Unable to get into the building's animal research facility, which they called, "an animal concentration camp," members of the group spray-painted corridors and laboratories and destroyed equipment. (February 1986)

■ A Macys department store in Manhattan was forced to lock its front doors for about one hour after a scuffle between customers and demonstrators who were protesting the use of animal furs in coats. The police issued 58 summons for disorderly conduct and charged one person with resisting arrest. (*New York Times*, March 22, 1985)

■ The United States Park Service police confiscated a Holstein calf from animal rights protesters who had used the animal in a demonstration outside the Department of Agriculture (USDA) building in Washington, D.C. The protest, conducted by a coalition of animal rights groups including the Fund for Animals and Farm Animal Reform Movement, was against the proposed USDA rules on branding of dairy cows to be bought by USDA. A USDA official said that police confiscated the calf, alleging failure to provide adequate shelter and care for the animal. Apparently, the calf was left locked in a vehicle on what was an unseasonably hot day, according to the National Association for Biomedical Research. (March 31, 1986)

■ Seven firebombs were left at a South London department store that sells fur coats, according to the *Daily Express*, a British newspaper. The Animal Liberation Front was responsible for the firebombs, according to the newspaper which cited information obtained by its own reporter during a three-month undercover assignment. The first-person account described meetings during which ALF members revealed plans to kidnap a member of the royal family, bomb the homes of scientists and doctors, burn research facilities to the ground, and terrorize the homes of certain police officers. In a front-page editorial accompanying the story, the newspaper called the activities of ALF "so close to terrorism... as to be indistinguishable from it." The newspaper reported that

Scotland Yard tracks ALF's activities daily, aided by computer information on more than 1,000 sympathizers. (May 5, 1986)

■ Farm Freedom Fighters claimed responsibility for liberating 25 laying hens from Sydel's Egg Farm in Hartly, Delaware. Members of the group spray-painted "Animal Auschwitz" and "FFF" on a farm building and left a note stating that there would be other "farm-animal liberation" actions in the United States. (June 4, 1986)

■ Using videotapes and photographs, animal rights activists have portrayed the eye injuries of a laboratory animal as evidence of abusive handling by scientists at the University of California, Riverside. A story, "Activists likely caused injuries to animals 'freed' from lab, report says," published by *The Atlanta Constitution*, quoted a National Institutes of Health Office for Protection from Research Risks report that the injuries must have occurred after the monkey was stolen from the university by the Animal Liberation Front. The newspaper story stated that "heavy bandages kept over the monkey's eyes apparently were removed by activists after the raid and replaced with thinner ones that didn't prevent the animal from scratching the sutures holding his eyelids shut. The eye [injuries] in the monkey, NIH said, probably were caused by the animal's post-raid scratching." (July 3, 1986)

■ California Attorney General John Van de Kamp submitted to the state Legislature a report on organized crime in California that identified the Animal Liberation Front as an active "terrorist group" in the state. (July 23, 1986)

■ The Animal Liberation Front stole 154 animals, including 100 rats and 26 rabbits, during a break-in at the University of Oregon at Eugene. Within days of the break-in, seven of the rabbits were found. According to the *Emerald,* an Oregon newspaper, the recovered rabbits required emergency medical care. In addition to the theft, vandalism caused more than $50,000 in damages, including the destruction of a $10,000 microscope. On December 30, 1986, animal rights activists held a press conference in Eugene, Oregon, and Los Angeles, California. According to the *Register-Guardian,* a Eugene newspaper, the "animal rights activists promised a bombshell at their news conferences... Their presentation was explosive, sure enough, but it blew up in their faces, damaging credibility that was already tattered by the burglary and vandalism of animal research laboratories at the University of Oregon." The press conferences were called to announce that ALF had photographs proving animal abuse, but the photos turned out to be prints from outdated instructional slides taken at another university. ALF admitted it found few cases violating the Animal Welfare Act at the university. In a letter sent to university officials and news media, ALF wrote that the break-in was designed "to demonstrate our unwillingness to accept the status quo of animal use and exploitation, even when carried out in compliance with established requirements of the law."

On July 10, 1987, a Portland, Oregon, man was arrested and charged with second-degree burglary, conspiracy to commit second-degree burglary, and first-degree theft in connection with the theft of the laboratory animals from the University of Oregon. Robert Smith Troen, 56, was charged with the three Class C felonies, each carrying penalties of up to five years in prison and up to $100,000 in fines. The indictment was obtained after police found three rabbits in the possession of an Oregon woman who told police that the rabbits had been stolen from the university. According to the *Sacramento Bee*, Troen is a self-described animal advocate. On March 24, 1988, Troen was convicted, fined $34,900, and sentenced to five years' probation by a judge who described the theft as an act of terrorism.

■ At Stanford University, police arrested 21 animal rights activists, including Elliot Katz, president of In Defense of Animals, for unlawful assembly, [refusal] to disperse and trespassing. Protesters blocked entrances to a university building. (November 10, 1986)

■ According to United Press International (UPI), "Demonstrators protesting the killing of animals for fur coats buttonholed shoppers and blocked store entrances in 43 cities... and 27 protesters were arrested." The UPI story quoted animal rights leader, George Cave, president of Trans-Species International, as stating: "Our primary focus is on the widespread institutionalized abuse of animals." (November 25, 1986)

■ An animal liberation group called True Friends stole four baby chimpanzees from SEMA, Inc., a medical research laboratory in Rockville, Maryland, that conducts scientific studies sponsored by the National Institute of Health. At a press conference in Washington, D.C., the People for the Ethical Treatment of animals incorrectly claimed the animals were to be "sealed into solid metal chambers in AIDS and hepatitis experiments." (December 7, 1986)

■ In Toronto, Canada, police arrested five people in connection with Animal Liberation Front break-ins and vandalism. According to the *Toronto Sun* newspaper, the arrests occurred when authorities caught three people spray-painting ALF slogans on a restaurant, while the other two waited in a nearby car that had been rented by the Toronto Humane Society. The Society denied involvement in the incident and told reporters that it did not support illegal activities.

■ A veterinary diagnostic center under construction at the University of California, Davis was destroyed by a fire that police believe was ignited by the Animal Liberation Front. The fire gutted the $10 million research facility that was intended to provide animal diagnostic services and disease surveillance. In addition to the fire, 18 university vehicles were vandalized. The letters "ALF" were painted on a wall. Lavonne Bishop of the Animal Rights Direct Action Coalition stated: "We don't condone violence, but we applaud the ALF... I'm glad they did it. I hope they do more of it." (April 16, 1987)

■ The Animal Liberation Front claimed responsibility for stealing more that 100 rabbits from a breeding farm in San Bernardino County. "ALF" and "Free the Bunnies" were painted on barn walls at the site of the crime. (April 18, 1987)

■ During a protest on World Day for Laboratory Animals, 17 members of the People for the Ethical Treatment of Animals were arrested when they refused to unchain themselves from the doors of the University of Arizona College of Medicine. Police officers used bolt cutters to sever the chains the protesters had wrapped and padlocked around their waists and the door exit bars. The 17 PETA members, who pled no contest, must serve six months of unsupervised probation and must either perform 10 hours of community work or pay a fine of $50. Other arrests for trespassing or unlawful assembly in connection with World Day for Laboratory Animals occurred at five universities in California and Cornell University in New York. (April 24, 1987)

■ Six horses were liberated from the Bureau of Land Management in Litchfield, California, by a group called the Western Wildlife Unit. (May 24, 1987)

■ According to the Fur Retailers Information Council, an incendiary device was hurled through a window of Hallmark Furs in St. Louis, Missouri, and caused more than $1 million in damages. In view of increasing violence and vandalism against the fur industry by animal rights protesters, animal rights advocates are suspected of being responsible for the incident. (June 2, 1987)

■ The Animal Liberation Front released five turkey vultures from the Raptor Center at the University of California, Davis. The Raptor Center specializes in research on, and the rehabilitation of, injured or sick wild birds. A handwritten note, signed by ALF and left at the facility, said: "Seven turkey vultures have been released. All records were searched. No more sacrifices." Three of the released birds were part of a study on the effect of compound 1080, a poison used to kill rodents such as ground squirrels. Two of the released birds were surrogate parents to other birds at the center. These birds were kept at the Raptor Center because of their inability to survive in the wild. The day after the break-in, one of the two birds whose cage had been opened but who had not escaped, died. All but one of the vultures released by ALF have been returned to the center. According to a researcher at the center, the birds were tame and easily recaptured by offers of food. They were hungry and had lost weight while free. (June 13, 1987)

■ The Band of Mercy stole 28 cats and seven African miniature pigs from the USDA's research center in Beltsville, Maryland. Eleven of the cats were being used in research on the prevention of infection by Toxoplasm gondii, a one-celled protozoan parasite that can be transmitted through feline feces to humans and other warm-blooded animals, and is responsible for birth defects in 3,000 children annually in the United States. According to *The New York Times,* the People for the Ethical Treatment of Animals acted as spokespersons for the Band of Mercy. (August 23, 1987)

■ During 1987, the Animal Liberation Front used incendiary devices in attacks on the homes and cars of researchers, butcher shops, farms, furriers, and department stores. In 1986, the ALF magazine published detailed instructions about the manufacture and assembly of these devices. In the United Kingdom, incidents involving firebombs rose from eight in 1985 to 32 in 1987. (1987)

■ The Animal Liberation Front stole 13 beagles from the University of California, Irvine. Eleven of the stolen animals were involved in painless research on the effects of air pollution on the lungs. Two of the dogs were used in a study on sleep apnea. (January 29, 1988)

■ Eight members of the Last Chance for Animals broke down a door in the Brain Research Institute at the University of California, Los Angeles. The activists were arrested and charged with felony burglary. Prior to the arrest, however, the activists managed to videotape themselves during the break-in. (April 21, 1988)

■ Animal Liberation Front members, Geoffrey Shepherd and Andrew Clarke, were sentenced to four and one-half years and three and one-half years respectively for their roles in firebomb attacks on Debenham's department store in England. (June 1988)

■ Seven people wearing dark clothing and carrying spray-paint cans were arrested by police at the University of California, Santa Cruz after their early morning animal-rights raid was interrupted by police. Slogans had been painted on numerous campus buildings and walk-ways. Three of those arrested had occupied a construction crane to protest animal research during an April 1988 protest. (September 24, 1988)

■ Fran Stephanie Trutt, Queens, New York, was charged with attempted murder and the manufacture and possession of bombs after police witnessed her placing bombs near the parking space of United States Surgical Company's president, Leon Hirsch. According to *Newsday*, Trutt said that she did not intend to harm Hirsch, but to cause property damage at the company because of its use of dogs in the development of surgical staples. "Property damage will cause an effect... All this guy [Hirsch] has to do is stop using live dogs... It's a very reasonable ultimatum. The odds of his effecting a change without a scare would be more likely to happen than if he were removed, so to speak, and someone else came into that position." (November 11, 1988)

■ Twelve animal rights activists were arrested at Emory University in Atlanta, Georgia, and charged with criminal trespass in connection with an In Defense of Animals staged protest against the university's Yerkes Regional Primate Research Center. The protest attracted 35 activists. Nine were arrested for blocking a driveway. Three were arrested in connection with hanging a banner titled, "Save the Yerkes Chimps," from a seven-story university building. The activists, experienced rock climbers, suspended themselves from ropes attached to the banner so that it could not be cut down. It took almost one hour for the local fire department to remove the three, one of whom was treated for mild hypothermia. (December 12, 1988)

■ The Animal Liberation Front claimed responsibility, in a telephone call to the Associated Press, for planting three packages with fake bombs at Stanford University. Attached to the first and only package to be discovered by police was a note to Dr. Thomas E. Hamm, the university's director of laboratory animal medicine, and his staff, that stated: "Have a bomb this Christmas." (December 24, 1989)

■ The Animal Liberation Front claimed responsibility for stealing four dogs from the Veterans Administration Medicine Center in Tucson, Arizona. ALF's statement to the news media, communicated by Tucson animal rights organization, Voices for Animals, stated that the "rights of these non-humans were going to be violated and that was sufficient reason to liberate them." (January 6, 1989)

■ An unidentified member of Earth First! telephoned the Associated Press and United Press International to claim responsibility for the fire that caused approximately $250,000 in damage at the Dixon Livestock Auction Company near Sacramento, California. The caller also claimed responsibility for vandalizing the Sacramento offices of the California Cattlemen's Association, California Wool Grower's Association, and the California Council on Agriculture. (January 29, 1989)

■ Eighteen animal rights activists were arrested at the University of California, Berkeley. Seven were arrested for climbing a 10-story construction crane and refusing to come down. Calling themselves the Coalition Against Militarism, Animal Abuse and Environmental hazards, the protesters vowed to remain on the crane until construction of the university's Northwest Animal Facility was halted. Construction of the facility was not affected, however, because the crane occupied by the activists was for the Genetics and Plant Biology Building. On February 24, four of the activists ended the sit-in and were arrested. Eleven were arrested for blocking a cement truck at the construction site. On the seventh day of the sit-in, the remaining activists on the crane descended, commenting that they were "getting tired and hungry and needed a shower." They were arrested for misdemeanor trespassing and released. University officials stated that the weekend-long sit-in cost the institution more than $200,000 in work delays and security. (February 1989)

■ Proclaiming to the media that "there is little need for knowledge that serves only human ends on the earth today the only honorable pursuit is that which promotes reverence for the sanctity of the earth and its inhabitants," the Animal Liberation Front stole 1,231 mice, rabbits, guinea pigs, frogs, and rats from the University of Arizona at Tucson. Damage from arson and vandalism totaled $250,000. In its news announcement, ALF also said it "conducted the liberation both as an act of mercy and compassion for the individual animal victims, and also as a part of a larger international campaign against the scientific/medical industry's misguided, anti-human, anti-earth, profit-oriented practices of vivisection, biotechnology and synthetic pharmaceutical research." The People for the Ethical Treatment of

Animals issued a news release stating that the liberated animals "have been placed in good homes." (April 3, 1989)

■ A San Francisco biotechnology company received a telephone threat by an individual who identified herself as an animal rights activist. According to *The San Francisco Chronicle,* the caller "threatened to stop the firm's research on a drug that makes pigs want to eat more." The newspaper quoted Chris DeRose, a spokesman for the Animal Liberation Front, as stating that, "threats and people possibly getting hurt" will not stop until "the research community stops factory farming and animal experiments." (April 12, 1989)

■ The Animal Liberation Front claimed responsibility for arson at a meat-packing firm in Monterey, California. According to the Monterey Fire Marshal, multiple incendiary devices were found that could have burned the building completely. ALF also vandalized walls and trucks with spray-painted graffiti. The Associated Press reported that a telephone caller to its San Francisco office stated that the fire was part of ALF's campaign to make "animal abuse... unprofitable. This is another strike in our campaign against an industry that slaughters billions of animals..." (April 28, 1989)

■ The scientific journal, *Nature,* reported that two laboratories of INSERM, the French National Institutes of Health and Medical Research at Lyons, France, were broken into and more than 40 macaque monkeys, 20 dogs, as well as cats, rabbits, and marsupials were stolen by the animal rights organization, Noah's Ark. The loss was estimated at $150,000. The evening after the break-in, national television news in France televised a videotape of the raid, recorded by the protesters. *Nature* reported that the INSERM laboratory may have been singled out for attack because of its links with Colin Blakemore, University of Oxford. Dr. Blakemore, a target of other attacks, had collaborated with the Lyons laboratory for the past 14 years. In a letter to the editor of *Nature,* Dr. Blakemore stated that the stolen monkeys included "social family groups that have been established for nearly a decade and animals that were born in the laboratory and had never experienced any other environment. Perhaps Hollands (a critic of animal research) would like to give us his opinion of the cruelty and stress involved in their forced removal and would tell us whether such treatment, without any scientific object at all, would be permitted under British law." (May 20, 1989)

■ The Animal Liberation Front claimed responsibility for releasing more than 600 birds owned by Chukars Unlimited, a hunters' group in Nevada, according to an Associated Press story. The story stated that the animal rights group botched the liberation when many of the birds were killed by passing cars. ALF also spray-painted "animals are friends, not food" messages on the walls of the Chukars Unlimited office. (June 2, 1989)

■ Avon evacuated its sales and distribution office in Atlanta, Georgia, after receiving a bomb threat from a caller identifying himself as a member of People for the Ethical Treatment of Animals. A search failed to uncover a bomb. A second phony call was received mid-afternoon. Avon spokesman, John Cox, commented: "We have tried, in good faith, not to deal with PETA. While ethics is one of their middle names, it is not one of their values." (June 5, 1989)

■ A *Washington Post* story, "Animal Research Labs Increasingly Are Under Siege," (May 30, 1989), featured a Northwestern University researcher who has been the subject of "death threats, bomb scares and a torrent of obscene phone calls from increasing militant activists committed to ending the use of laboratory animals in medical research." According to the story, scientists who conduct research with animals at Johns Hopkins University, Duke Medical Center, Harvard University, the National Institutes of Health, and Cornell University "have all received death threats in the past year." In the article, Ingrid Newkirk, national director of PETA, stated: "It's immoral even if it's [animal research study is] essential... If my father had a heart attack it would give me no solace at all to know his treatment was first tried on a dog." In a speech at the University of Chicago, United States Health and Human Services Undersecretary Constance Horner said that pharmaceutical firms are "closing down research into new drugs" because of personal threats by the animal rights activists. Horner said that their effect on research is now largely unnoticed because the drug companies are not publicizing their actions. (June 14, 1989)

■ The Animal Liberation Front broke into a research laboratory and office at Texas Tech University Health Sciences Center in Lubbock. An estimated $50,000 to $70,000 worth of equipment was destroyed; five cats trained in sleep research were stolen; and, research data and a scientist's personal documents were stolen. The cats were involved in research, sponsored by the National Heart, Lung and Blood Institute, dealing with breathing during sleep. (July 4, 1989)

This ends the lengthy list of incidents taken from the court records of the Berosini case.

Despite beefed-up security at campuses and businesses across the country and around the world, the demonstrations and destructions continue. English activists are getting busier and bolder. In June 1990, a car bomb injured a veterinarian and an animal rights group admitted to trying to kill her. Less than a week earlier, a bomb detonated underneath the car of a Bristol researcher, injuring a 13-month-old child in a carriage nearby (the child had shrapnel wounds, burns and a partially severed finger). Talk radio callers are beginning to publicly urge death to specific researchers.

At home, a June 1991 fire destroyed mink-feed warehouses in Edmonds, Washington. In the same month, an experimental mink research facility was also torched at Oregon State University.

The Spring/1992 issue of *MSU Today* reported that the Animal Liberation Front broke into Michigan State University's Anthony Hall. Two animal science faculty members had a cumulative total of 42 years of research destroyed. Animal science professor, Richard Aulerich, lead researcher in Michigan State University's mink and associated toxicology research was the prime target. His neighbor in Anthony Hall was Karen Chou, an assistant professor and toxicology expert. Aulerich's 32 years of information, publications, grant proposals, notebooks and other data were piled on his floor and set on fire. Chou's 10 years of files, which included information she had collected for a book, were lost in the heat of the fire. Others lost files, records and personal items, also. The cost of the damage at Anthony Hall was estimated at $50,000.

A Michigan State University mink research facility was vandalized the same night,resulting in $25,000 in damages and the loss of two mink. The People for the Ethical Treatment of Animals issued a press release on the ALF raid that accused Aulerich of killing thousands of mink in painful and scientifically useless experiments.

Ironically, the mink and toxicology research beneficiaries are both humans and mink in the areas of toxicology and deafness research. Aulerich chairs the All-University Committee on Animal Use, which oversees all research projects using animals and insures compliance with federal guidelines for humane care. Assistant Professor Chou's reaction to the raid: "I want people who give to PETA to understand that their money is doing the opposite of what they intend."

In October, 1992, US Department of Agriculture research offices connected to a predator research center at Utah State University were torched. More than $200,000 in damages occurred and about 12 coyotes were released.

On November 8, 1992, five meat trucks in Minneapolis were painted with "ALF," "Meat is Murder," and destroyed by firebombing, causing $100,000 damages.

The raids, disruptions, acts of violence and destruction, legislative forays and media moralizing cross the board as they relate to human's use of animals. Look in any direction and you can see the continued push to eliminate the use of animals in any form. The methods are unlimited: whatever works. ⊕

# SECTION IV
# CONCLUSION

# ⊞ CHAPTER 10. Taking the Initiative

*The worst sin towards our fellow creatures is not to hate them, but to be indifferent to them. That is the essence of inhumanity.*
George Bernard Shaw, quoted from page 1 of Newkirk's *Save the Animals! 101 Things You Can Do*

*7th Satanic statement: Satan represents man as just another animal, sometimes better, more often worse than those that walk on all four, who because of his "divine spiritual and intellectual development" has become the most vicious of all.*
Satanic Bible

*Hitler had the best of all ideas.*
Charles Manson

In August 1992, President Bush signed The Farm Animal and Research Facilities Protection Act into law, making animal terrorism, sabotage and animal release (liberation) federal crimes. A few months earlier, grand juries convened in Michigan, Washington and Oregon and PETA's founders were subpoenaed to appear as part of a federal investigation into the activities of ALF. The power of the federal government, the Department of Justice, the FBI and the United States Bureau of Alcohol, Tobacco and Firearms had at last been brought to bear on the extremist wing of the animal rights movement. All across the country people involved with animal issues heaved a collective sigh of relief.

Students of the animal rights movement aren't quite ready to relax, however. They realize that the movement is driven by something that has always been outside the control of government agencies and laws. In stark contrast to the 19th Century humane movement that was founded out of idealism and compassion, the cult of animal rights is fueled by cynicism. It capitalizes on the fact that people today feel overwhelmed and helpless in the face of staggering problems for which they have no answers. They are sickened and immobilized by images that show the progressive destruction of the natural world, and are afraid of annihilation through other people's misguided use of increasingly complex technology and science. Animalism draws its power from its ability to exploit compassion while amplifying this sense of cynicism and hopelessness. It thereby aligns itself with hatred rather than love for humanity. People who have been targets of animalism know that hatred is its driving force and understand that it requires regular feeding.

Human sacrifice has always accompanied animal worship. Today, as in the Nazi era, disillusionment, despair and cynicism are features of the time; they pave the way for new doctrines and political movements that pander to human fears. In German Nazism, the metaphysics of hate were starkly clear. But the version of animalism practiced in England and America, whether centered on individual animals (pets and lab animals for example), or clothed in the larger religion of environmentalism, is not so easily discerned. In German Nazism an identifiable segment of humanity served as the scapegoat. In the modern version, however, the scapegoat target is so immense that the public has trouble grasping its scope: It's the entire human race. It's hard for the public to believe that when Mitchell Fox of PAWS says that because of humans, pet slaughter goes on, or when Michael Fox of HSUS says that human nature is the problem, or when Ingrid Newkirk of PETA says that humans are the biggest blight on the face of the earth, or when Dave Foreman of Earth First! says that humanity is the cancer of nature and he is the antibody that they are sharing the very core of their belief system. The animal rights and environmental biocentrics (deep ecologists included) collectively represent a hate movement that is disillusioned with, and "tired of," the entire human race. These fanatics identify with animals, projecting their feelings of helplessness onto them while they, through some sad route, have disconnected from their own species.

The animalists' answer to human pain, like the German Nazi answer, is to get people to focus on their differences rather than on what they have in common. It encourages moral one-upmanship and convinces people that some may be sacrificed on moral grounds, defined by animalists, without damaging the whole.

Their answer denies a vital component of human development. Compassion grows out of experience in the world. Many children, and not just ones who wind up in prison, but also those who grow up to compose beautiful music, to perform heart transplants and those who leap into rivers to save drowning children start out examining insects by pulling their wings off. Many who grow to be wonderful pet owners learned from a starting attitude that wasn't ideal for their animals.

The animal rights movement, in its manipulation of contemporary cynicism and disgust with man's imperfect path of growth and development, not only forces humanity to focus on the empty portion of the half-full glass, but also relentlessly demands that everyone must remain transfixed by the empty half. Albert Einstein once offered that the most important question for mankind is: "Is the universe friendly?" That is, if the pre-existing assumptions about the world (or the part of it being studied) are not, as he termed it, "friendly," and if the half-full glass is viewed as half empty, then the proposed solutions to problems would lead only to more problems. He was saying that solutions that are driven by negative emotions such as fear, anger and hatred provide destructive responses to problems. He was acknowledging that if we don't focus on what we love, we risk losing everything. The pre-existing assumption in animal rights' philosophy is not only that the universe is unfriendly, but also that humans made it that way.

Albert Schweitzer is revered as a humanitarian by people everywhere. The rightists claim him for their own by making him a hero and human banner of sorts for the animal rights movement. As a vegetarian, humanitarian, one who was devoted to living as a participant in the world environment, and who contributed to human development and the alleviation of suffering, any group would be proud of such an association. The animal rights leaders, however, in appropriating his image leave out something very important about Schweitzer's ethic when they use him to promote their cause. Schweitzer recognized that for humans or any other organisms, merely existing had an impact on the rest of the environment, sometimes in positive ways and sometimes negative.

When asked whether his reverence for all life contradicted killing other life forms, he answered with an illustration to show concern for the necessity of the act and responsibility for the life taken:

The farmer who has mowed down a thousand flowers in his meadow in order to feed his cows must be careful on his way home not to strike the head off a single flower by the side of the road in idle amusement, for he thereby infringes the law of life without being under the pressure of necessity.

Schweitzer approved of killing animals for medical research, but under the same conditions that the contemporary biomedical community requires: a proven need and humane sacrifice.

Schweitzer observed that the "'sacrifice' of a life for humanity, created an obligation for everyone 'to do as much good as we possibly can to all creatures in all sorts of circumstances.'" Schweitzer would rescue struggling insects, but he was also aware of the inescapable need for humanity to survive, and grow in the present. Hence, taking an experimental animal's life when necessary and raising cattle were considered to be acceptable practices while en route to an existence that could enjoy maximum appreciation and reverence for all things, living and non-living. His understanding of the need to affirm human life is clear.

The animal rights movement misses entirely the need for living in the present as evidenced by its demand for immediate compliance to the leaders' ethical position of complete separation from animals. The movement's position ignores the fact that each individual is traveling his own ethical course of development (a belief central to both Eastern and Western religions) which if interrupted, like omitting a stage of creeping or crawling en route to walking, may block one's ability to reach the state of compassion necessary to maintain one's own delicate humanity. People from such diverse backgrounds as: Karl Menninger, psychiatrist; George T. Angell, founder of the Massachusetts SPCA; and other great men, such as Gandhi, Schweitzer and Martin Luther King Jr., have all recognized that our ability to grow more compassionate diminishes in the absence of experience which requires it. Carl Jung pointed out: "Neurosis is always a substitute for legitimate suffering." And Stevie Wonder's lyrics enjoin: "You can't be in it but not of it."

This is in stark contrast to Ingrid Newkirk's somber confession: "I am not a morose person, but I would rather not be here. I don't have any reverence for life, only for the entities themselves. I

— 132 —

would rather see a blank space where I am. This will sound like fruitcake stuff again but at least I wouldn't be harming anything. All I can do—all you can do—while you are alive is try to reduce the amount of damage you do by being alive." In Jonestown, where a cult-led, self-inflicted massacre of hundreds of men, women and children occurred, a similar conclusion was reached and recently a hunting magazine reported that an animalist had suggested mass suicide as a way out of this dilemma.

Earth First! founder Dave Foreman's response to famine also illustrates the difference: "The worst thing we could do in Ethiopia is give aid... The best thing would be to just let nature seek its own balance, to let people there just starve." In an echo of Newkirk's quote, he also offered: "The human race could go extinct and I for one would not shed any tears." And, as a partial solution for overpopulation: "AIDS is a good thing, because it will thin out the population... If the AIDS epidemic didn't exist, radical environmentalists would have to invent one."

The missing element in the animalist philosophy is *compassion for human suffering*. According to George Bernard Shaw, another banner carrier appropriated for the movement: "The worst sin towards our fellow creatures is not to hate them, but to be indifferent to them. That is the essence of inhumanity." But the animalists contradict this great playwright. They suggest that in the face of human suffering we should look the other way. We should let people starve, stop seeking cures, ignore crippled children, and let nature—Gaia—seek its balance. It is clear that animalists, as in the seventh satanic statement represent "man as just another animal, sometimes better, more often worse than those that walk on all four, who because of his 'divine spiritual and intellectual development' has become the most vicious of all."

Animal rights literature is full of articles that urge compassion toward the unheeded cries of animals under human dominion. Yet, they condemn researchers who hear and feel compelled to answer another cry. These priorities appall the research community because, as Dr. Adrian Morrison, a researcher who has had his work disrupted by animal extremists explains: "What animal can match in suffering the heartbreak of parents, who lose a child to illness or have given birth to a child with severe birth defects, or the despair of a teenager who learns that life in the future will be incomplete as a result of the car accident that severed his spinal cord? Even Chimpanzees, I understand, can not participate in the grief of others. We can, even when learning of a tragedy in the newspaper. This makes us special." Morrison's understanding of what makes humans special is not arrogant, as animalists assert, but is based on his belief in humanity's unique gift of compassion.

Presbyterian minister and educator Robert McAfee Brown enlarges on this understanding in a tribute to a friend. Brown exhorts the human need to strive toward utopia while being forced to live in a world that includes pain and suffering, urging that "while the goal is too vast to be realized solely on this planet, it is still our task to create foretastes of it on this planet—living glimpses of what life is *meant* to be, which include art and music and poetry and shared laughter and picnics and moral outrage and special privileges for children only and wonder and humor and endless love, to counterbalance the otherwise immobilizing realities of tyrants, starving children, death camps and just plain greed."

Our own humanity is defined by our choice to sacrifice the comfort of indifference or the expediency of hate in order to comfort and serve others in the face of overwhelming pressures to do otherwise.

* * * *

**Who is speaking for reason? Who is willing to fight this threat?**

Many groups have organized to expose and oppose the extremists in the animal and environmental movements. There are single-issue groups with interests in such areas as livestock, fur, pharmaceuticals, hunting, trapping, pet-owning, pet-breeding, purebred breeding, training, as well as other animal-related pursuits. There are groups involved in a general range of interest, such as hunting, fishing and trapping. There are full-spectrum groups which may have medicine at one end and trapping at the other, groups that lobby, activist groups, and groups that serve as resource and research entities. While there are many excellent single-issue organizations and organizations that serve specialized functions, this book will introduce just a few organizations who have good track records for connecting interested parties with further resources. (For addresses of these organizations, please see Appendix.)

The **National Animal Interest Alliance** (NAIA) is based in Portland, Oregon. NAIA is a national umbrella organization representing veterinarians, sports enthusiasts, biomedical researchers, pet owners and animal breeders, as well as agricultural, entertainment and business interests. These entities fully support and promote animal welfare, but are adamantly opposed to animal rights. Co-author Patti Strand, executive director of NAIA, has established a national mutual support network from a wide range of business, scientific, professional and personal-interest areas. The organization is a resource for both media and individuals wanting to learn more about the political agendas and practices of the radical animal and environmental groups. It offers a newsletter and will provide speakers, writers and experts in a number of different animal-related specialties for interested parties, including the media.

Strand has spoken on radio and television shows regarding animal-rights issues. She has also given national-level presentations at professional, scientific and sporting conventions.

Before writing this book, both Strand, and her husband Rod, had written more than 40 articles for national publications in an effort to get information to the public on this subject. NAIA offers support, through providing information and factual data to groups and individuals who are being targeted by any animal extremists. NAIA's specialty is researching studies and working with subject matter experts to provide factual information on issues that are either unknown or confusing to the public. NAIA's board is comprised of animal experts from a wide range of backgrounds.

**Putting People First** (PPF), based in Washington, D.C., was started by Kathleen Marquardt in reaction to what her children were being taught about animal rights in the school system. PPF has counterattacked the animal rights agenda in the media, through public presentations, lobbying efforts and by tracking and reporting animal rights activities as they occur. It was among the first organizations to take a public position against the terrorism and hidden agenda of the animal rights movement. It publishes two informative publications: *From the Trenches,* a newsletter, and *The People's Agenda,* a newspaper. Press Secretary Mark LaRochelle has done excellent research and writing for both publications.

The **American Animal Welfare Foundation** (AAWF) in St.

Paul, Minnesota, is a full-spectrum group which also has animal experts on their board. Program Director Marcia Kelly is one of the top animal rights experts in the country. Her organization works as an information resource to alert the public to the difference between animal rights and animal welfare. AAWF was among the first to recognize the flawed value system that forms the basis for the animal rights agenda.

The **Americans for Medical Progress** (AMP), located in Arlington, Virginia, maintains volumes of information about medical progress using animal research. Because animal research is under attack, it also has information on the animal rights movement and animal-rights-related organizations. It is a group formed to support biomedical research through educating the public about the benefits that have come from animal research. Executive Director Susan Paris runs an organization that serves as a helpful resource for anyone seeking educational material and background information on these and related subjects.

The **Coalition for Animals & Animal Research** (CFAAR), has branches in several locations across the country. CFAAR is another animal research support organization. Educating the public about the benefits of research is its primary function. Patrick Cleveland, of the San Diego branch, is one of the nation's top experts on the subject of animal rights and has written some excellent articles for the CFAAR newsletter. Sharon Russell, in Berkeley, is another outstanding CFAAR researcher and contributor. As an organization with academic leanings, CFAAR monitors animal rights propaganda in the schools. The CFAAR newsletter contains information and perspectives on the broad-based, continuing assault of animal rights extremists against education and research across the country.

The **Foundation for Biomedical Research** is a group whose mission is to improve the quality of animal and human health by promoting public understanding and support of the ethical use of animals in scientific and medical research. For more information, contact Mary Brennan, vice president.

**Incurably Ill for Animal Research** (IIFAR) is the nation's only patient-based animal research advocacy organization. Its primary mission is public education regarding the positive contributions of animal research. Charles Sheaffer is the person to contact there.

These are just a few of the national groups, but each one

contains leading national experts on their subjects who share their resources with people who need help.

Throughout this book, the authors have attempted to explain the nature and origin of the animal rights movement, its belief system, its structure, mode of operation and political alliances. Many people question the importance of the movement because the number of activist leaders around the country is small. Many others may feel they can finally relax because there has been movement in the direction of anti-terrorist legislation and because the legal system has taken the initiative against the threat. Moreover, many people believe that once the top four or five major players are locked up the problem will end. They are wrong on all counts.

There are still many reasons to remain alert. One big reason is that despite the small number of leaders, their distorted and hateful rhetoric was able to find fertile soil. There are ten million followers of the animal rights movement and hundreds of millions of dollars that have been donated to this cause in America. That in itself should frighten the daylights out of anyone with a background in history. It's a call to widespread public participation in government, a notice to citizens everywhere to learn the facts about animal and environmental issues and to get involved with the process to begin actively monitoring and helping to develop public policy.

Next, in the English experience, terrorism actually escalated after Ronnie Lee was sent to jail. Here too, the layered and dispersed cell structure of the movement assures that if major leaders wind up in jail, new leader-activists, probably already designated, will take over their roles and carry on the *war* as though nothing happened. There is also the worry that the movement is growing more cult-like; cult expert Shirley Landa says that many of these groups "share a growing acceptance of 'the seductive premise,' common to many cults, which in this instance, can lead to 'animals over people'" Furthermore, if the radical fringe quiets down, the plentiful propaganda already existing in schools and popular culture could pass uncontested into mainstream acceptance, giving animalists even more political clout to enact their world view. That is exactly where we are today.

Although the animal rights movement may seem like an inconsequential speck on the modern landscape of social change, it is an important element because it offers close-up glimpses of new, radical strategies and tactics that support some rather well-known older goals. By acting as protectors of the voiceless constituents of animals and other natural world elements, they have gained access to the democratic process as agents for a group whose identity it then confuses with legitimate minorities. Through adopting an agency role that uses our own evolving liberal traditions, compassion for animals and cynicism for humanity, they are able to bypass the democratic process and gain power.

The goals of the left have not changed since long before the time when Kim Stallwood first decided to link up with the *new-left* coalition that was being forged in England in the 70s. It's no coincidence that enactment of the so-called animal agenda (see Appendix) results in outcomes desired by the *old left* as well. Interestingly, at the summer 1992 Rio de Janeiro environmental summit, the new environmental goals turned out to be key elements of the old socialist party platform that have been around for dozens of years. It turns out you truly can't give an animal rights without first taking them away from people.

Their efforts are currently directed in four main areas:

1. *The dissolution of private property:* In the political sphere, watch all activities that have the possibility of removing either property or property-user rights. Nothing removes private property as quickly as the endangered species laws (biodiversity), but regulating away users' rights (which makes private property irrelevant) is a close runner-up.

2. *Promoting the substitution of monotheistic (hierarchical) religions by pantheistic (egalitarian) religions:* By trying to replace Christianity, Judaism and Islam with a nature-oriented one, environmentalism is rapidly becoming the dominant religion of the age. Sunday morning cartoons, such as Captain Planet, movies such as *FernGully* and the new G.I. Joe Eco-Warriors point to common acceptance of the new religion.

3. *Propagandizing youth:* The next generation is being

bombarded with messages from animal rightists and biocentric environmentalists in schools all over America. Sometimes the vehicle for entry into the school is an instructor who is in favor of animal rights; sometimes it is a newsletter or paraphernalia from outside the system, such as trusted information sources like encyclopedias and weekly readers. The typical message exalts nature for its perfection and innocence while demoralizing and dehumanizing kids because humans are to blame for everything that is wrong in the world. Schools are loaded with animal rights material that can use the doubts and insecurities of youth to instill the kind of misinformation that distorts animal use and magnifies disenchantment with humanity.

4. *Creating legislative inroads:* The pressure on federal, state and local lawmakers to pass laws that favor the animal rights agenda is complemented by continuous pressure to appoint administrators and regulators who favor animal rights concepts. At all levels, watch the expressions of interest in administrative decision making and demand a factual basis and representative support for proposed actions. Watch the agencies that deal with animal and environmental issues, and watch for shifts in jurisdiction from one department to another (one of the animal rights' agenda goals is to remove animal authority from the Department of Agriculture).

**What can you do about the animal extremism?**
First and foremost, you must watch where you send your contributions, and demand specific, written explanations of how your money will be used and what results are anticipated. Make sure that every dollar you donate to a cause espousing concern for animals is as directly effective as it would be if you were to adopt an animal from a shelter, pay for a spaying or neutering operation, or personally print and distribute educational information to the public.

With the understanding that the school system is also under attack, you should scrutinize your children's educational materials to make sure that they're not promoting a belief system that values animals at levels equal to, or above human beings. You should also share documented information about animal extremism with your school administration if you get responses from officials that indicate a lack of awareness on this subject.

Carefully investigate areas of animal concern. Keep in mind that most people no longer have hands-on experience with animals. Recognize that the knowledge you have, if obtained second-hand, may not be accurate. Understand that information that comes to you may be intended to manipulate your perception of the situation. Find information provided by expert resources, especially with regard to animal users who are accused in the media of abusive practices. Remember that news reports often use the *sizzle* of information provided by parties who have specific messages to get across to the public. Don't blindly accept second-hand information as truth. Contact directly the subjects of negative news reports or private mailings for their sides of the issues. If you're willing to donate $5 to a cause, you should be willing to spend $2.50 on a phone call to the accused or to an expert resource. Use your own good judgment to determine the truth.

And don't stop there. Find other experts in the field, especially those who aren't asking for your money, to clarify the situation. There are plenty of sources: businesses, universities, libraries, professional societies, and special-interest groups. Giving even one dollar blindly without having at least three sources of information from different perspectives and knowing the exact disposition of the donation is like throwing gasoline on a fire. In the absence of this information, you may literally be contributing to an organization determined to keep the fire going.

When you have enough information to consider yourself better informed than the average person, use it and share it. Use it by demanding accountability in every area relating to environmental and animal issues. Each individual who communicates about these issues has a responsibility to insure that the information is accurate. Television, radio and print media reporters have this same responsibility, but it is your task to hold them to a critical standard of accuracy. Share your findings with family, friends, the news media, talk show hosts, and public officials. Write to your political representatives and establish a relationship with staff members who specialize in the area of animal issues. One of the reasons for the success of animal extremism is that the targets tend to feel so isolated, amazed and depressed at the public's misunderstanding of their work that they don't communicate with others. Sharing information not only gets to the heart of the issue, it breaks down barriers of silence.

At some point in your investigation, you will discover a language of animal-rights-activism jargon used to reinforce the tendency toward uncritical examination of animal rights issues. Examine your own speech and get rid of this jargon. Watch what you're saying and understand the possible hidden meanings, importance and effect of the words you choose to explain things.

Finally, in keeping with King's exhortation that "to ignore evil is to become an accomplice to it," follow Frederick K. Goodwin's advice quoted in "An Open Letter to the Research Community" written as director for the National Institute of Alcohol, Drug Abuse and Mental Health:

> Passivity sets up people to give in to their fears, to become victims... We know that in the animal kingdom, when an animal is faced with a predator, the worst thing that an animal can do is freeze. The best thing the animal can do is scream, like the monkeys do, and adopt an aggressive posture. ⊞

# SECTION V.
# REFERENCE MATERIAL

# CHAPTER NOTES

**Acknowledgments**

page ii.     The authors wish to thank Sherrie Hicks and Ron Calhoun, Partners in Research, for passing along these wonderfully appropriate quotes.

**In the Beginning...**

page x.     From an article titled "Animal Rights, Militancy and Terrorism," printed in *Information Digest* (April 1991, Vol. XXIV #7, Baltimore) by John and Louise Rees.

**Chapter 1**

page 1.     From James Serpell's book, *In the Company of Animals* (Blackwell, 1986), pp 3-5.

page 2.     From the book, *Origins*, by R.E. Leaky and R. Lewin (MacDonald & Jane's, London, 1977), pp 123, 142-147.

page 2.     From the U. S. Dept. of Agriculture, Economic Research Service.

page 2.     From Stephen Dubiansky's book, *The Covenant of the Wild, Why Animals Chose Domestication* (William Morrow and Company, Inc., 1992), p 3. This book is an excellent resource for anyone seeking more understanding and a different perspective on current animal issues.

page 3.     From the *World Book Encyclopedia* P15, 1990 Edition, pp 675-677.

page 5.     From *The Inhumane Society* by Dr. Michael W. Fox (St. Martins Press, 1990), p 4.

page 6.     From *Men, Beasts, and Gods* by Gerald Carson (Charles Scribner's Sons, New York, 1972), p 3-12.

page 6.     From James Parker's book, *Man and Beast He*

*Preserves, Humans and Animals in the Bible and Jewish and Christian Traditions* (Parker, 1991), pp 1-23. Copies of this excellent resource are available for $5, prepaid, sent to: James Parker, 4327 NE Glisan St., Portland, OR 97213.

      page 6.     From the Parker book.

      page 7.     Animal rightists' behavior is more right wing in operation than left, but their agendas for change share similar priorities.

      page 9.     From an article by Katie McCabe titled "Who Will Live Who Will Die," printed in *Washingtonian Magazine*, August/1986, p 115. This quote is taken from the undisputed portion of Ms. McCabe's article.

      page 9.     From the Parker book, p 2.

      page 9.     From Peter Singer's book, *Animal Liberation, A New Ethics for our Treatment of Animals* (New York Review Book, 1975), p 202. Anyone who wants to understand how animal rights and the Judeo-Christian belief system relate, should read Singer's book. If time is a factor, at least read Chapter 5, "Man's Dominion...A Short History of Speciesism."

      page 11.    From an interview with Paul Watson by Dean Kuipers (*Andy Warhol's Interview Magazine*, August 1992) titled "Pirates with a Difference," p 94.

      page 12.    From *The Rights of Nature, a History of Environmental Ethics* by Roderick Frazier Nash (The University of Wisconsin Press, 1989), p 194.

      page 12.    From the article, "Animal Rights, Militancy and Terrorism," published in *Information Digest* (April 1991, Vol. XXIV, #7, Baltimore), written by John and Louise Rees.

## Chapter 2

      page 14.    From *Men, Beasts, and Gods*, by Gerald Carson (Charles Scribner's Sons, New York, 1972), p 49.

      page 14.    From *All Heaven in a Rage* by E. S. Turner (St. Martin's Press, New York, 1964), p 74.

      page 14.    From the Turner book, p 35.

      page 15.    From the Turner book, p 33.

      page 15.    From the Carson book, p 37.

      page 15.    From the Turner book, p 55.

page 16.  From the Turner book, pp 45, 46.
page 16.  From the Carson book, p 61.
page 16.  From *The Rights of Nature* by Roderick Frazier Nash (University of Wisconsin Press, 1989), p 26.
page 17.  From the Turner book, pp 40, 41.
page 17.  From the Turner book, pp 156-160.
page 17.  From the Turner book, pp 119-130.
page 18.  From the Carson book, p 45.
page 19.  From the Turner book, p 209.
page 19.  From *The Human Mind* by Karl Menninger.
page 20.  From "The Animal Rights War on Medicine," printed in *Reader's Digest*, June 1990, p 72.
page 20.  From the Carson book, pp 103-106.
page 21.  From the Turner book, p 160.
page 21.  From the Carson book, pp 107-112.
page 22.  From the Nash book, p 42.
page 23.  From an article, "The Development of the Animal Protection Movement," by Andrew Rowan, printed in *The Journal of NIH Research*, November/December 1989, p 97.
page 24.  From the Turner book, p 166.

**Chapter 3**

page 26.  From an article titled "The Animal Rights War on Medicine" by John G. Hubbell, printed in *Reader's Digest*, June 1990, p 72.
page 26.  From James V. Parker's book, *Man and Beast He Preserves*, (Portland, Parker, 1991), p 11.
page 26.  From an article titled "Understanding Nazi Animal Protection and the Holocaust" by Arnold Arluke and Boria Sax, printed in *Anthrozoos*, Vol. 5 No. 1 (1992), pp 7-8.
page 26.  From the Arluke and Sax article, pp 19-20.
page 27.  From *The Goebbels Diaries 1939-1941*, by Fred Taylor (G.P. Putnam's Sons, New York, 1983), p 77.
page 29.  From an article by John and Louise Rees titled, "Animal Rights: Militancy and Terrorism," printed in *Information Digest*, June 5, 1991, p 5.
page 29.  From the Taylor book, p 36.
page 29.  From the Taylor book, p 77.

page 31.  From *Animal Warfare* by David Henshaw (William Collins Sons & Co. Ltd., Glasgow, 1989), p 191.

## Chapter 4

page 33.  From Peter Singer's book, *Animal Liberation*, preface, vii.

page 33.  From *Animal Warfare: The Story of the Animal Liberation Front* by David Henshaw (Fontana Paperbacks, London, 1989) , p 122.

page 33.  From the Henshaw book, p 160.

page 34.  From the Henshaw book, p 11.

page 35.  From the Henshaw book, p 195.

page 35.  From the Henshaw book, p 52, and from Glenn C. Schoen's piece titled "Terrorists or Common Criminals," printed in *Counterterrorism & Security*, Winter 89/90.

page 36.  From a booklet by David T. Hardy, Esq. titled "America's New Extremists: What You Need to Know About the Animal Rights Movement," printed by the Washington Legal Foundation, Washington, D.C., 1990, p 20.

page 37.  From the Henshaw book, pp 12-20; 203-203.

page 38.  From the Henshaw book,  pp 203-204, and Schoen.

page 40.  From  the Henshaw book, p 160.

page 41.  From the Henshaw book, pp 160-162.

page 41.  From the Henshaw book, pp 158-171.

page 42.  From the Schoen piece.

page 42.  From the Fox book, p 4.

page 43.  From an article titled "Just Like Us?" by Arthur Caplan, et al., printed in *Harpers*, August 1988, p 50.

page 43.  From *The Daily Californian*, February 9, 1989. The article was quoting Dr. Barnard's address to an audience at the International House at Berkeley.

page 43.  From the Singer book, p 9.

page 44.  From the Hardy piece, p 25-26.

page 45.  From an address by Cleveland Amory, Reed College, Portland, Or, 1991.

page 45.  From an article in the *Village Voice* titled "The Ugly Secret of Black Beauty Ranch," 1991.

page 47. From "Holding the Radical Line" in *USA Today* by Carolyn Pesce.

page 48. The *amicus* brief submitted on behalf of Bobby Berosini in the appeal brought by PETA #21580: Appeal from the Judgment of the Eighth Judicial District Court, Clark County, Nevada. This brief was prepared by David Hardy, Esq., of the Washington Legal Foundation. Hardy, in addition to preparing this brief (which contains superb foundation information with supporting documentation), has also written a booklet on the animal rights movement, which is an excellent resource, "America's New Extremists." Everyone writing on this subject today can thank him for much of the original research. The authors are in his debt and also in the debt of the organization, Putting People First, for signing on the brief as *amicus curiae*.

page 48. From an article by Howard Rosenberg titled "To Market, To Market," printed in the *Los Angeles Times Magazine*, March 22, 1992, p 22.

page 48. From the Carolyn Pesce article.

page 48. From the *Washington Post*, November 13, 1983.

page 48. From *Vogue*, September 1989.

page 48. From *Washingtonian Magazine*, August 1986.

page 49. From *Amicus* Brief No. 21580, p 10.

page 51. *American Medical Association*, March 12, 1992.

page 51. From *Information Digest* (Vol. XXIV, No. 7), April 5, 1991, p 20.

page 53. From PETA, PAWS, ALF, by Shirley Landa, p 2.

page 53. From *American Medical Association*, 1992, and *Information Digest*, May 5, 1991, p 10.

page 54. From the Fox book, p 245.

## Chapter 5

page 60. From an article by Kathleen Marquardt titled "Green With Envy," printed in *From the Trenches* (Putting People First, Washington, D.C.) November 18, 1992, p 1.

page 60. From the Katie McCabe article "Who Will Live, Who Will Die?" printed in *The Washingtonian*, August 1986, p 116.

page 68. From the Peter Singer book.

page 68.    From "Students United Protesting Research on Sentient Subjects," Pasadena, California.

page 71.    From the *San Mateo Times*, San Mateo, California, December 18, 1985.

## Chapter 6

page 81.    From an interview with Steve Medina, July 1992.

page 81.    From a publication by the National Academy of Sciences titled, *Dolphins and the Tuna Industry* (National Academy Press, Washington, 1992), p 4.

page 82.    From the National Academy Press, pp 5-27.

page 83.    From the Medina interview.

page 84.    From an interview with Teresa Platt, co-director of the Fisherman of the Eastern Tropical Pacific Ocean, August 1992.

page 86.    From the National Academy Press, p 49.

page 88.    From the IATTC Review Panel, established April 23, 1992, which includes Colombia, Costa Rica, Ecuador, Mexico, Panama, Spain, Vanuatu, Venezuela, and the United States.

## Chapter 7

page 90.    From "Silver Springs Monkeys." Videos available from PETA: flier.

page 90.    From *State of Maryland vs. Edward Taub* (Montgomery County Dist. Ct. #111848-81) 1981.

page 91.    From an article by Sharon M. Russell titled "The Silver Spring Monkey Story: Summary Update and Epilogue," printed in the *Coalition for Animals & Animal Research*, Winter/Spring, 1991, p10.

page 91.    From an article by Edward Taub, Ph.D. titled "The Silver Spring Monkey Incident: The Untold Story," printed in *Coalition for Animals & Animal Research*, Winter/Spring, 1991.

page 92.    From court records, *State of Maryland vs. Edward Taub*, #111848-81.

page 94.    From an article by Joseph Palca titled "Famous Monkeys Provide Surprising Results," printed in *Science*, June 28,

1991, p 1789.

page 95. From personal interviews with Dr. Edward Taub, September-December, 1992.

page 95. From Taub interviews.

page 95. From a personal interview with Dr. Adrian Morrison, February 1992.

**Chapter 8**

page 97. From a personal interview with Bobby and Joan Berosini, October 1991.

page 98. From *Berousek a.k.a. Berosini vs. People for the Ethical Treatment of Animals*, District Court, Clark County, Nevada, September 11, 1991, case #A276505.

page 99. From an article by Phil Herschkop titled "Absence of Malice: The Berosini Trial," printed in *PETA News*, November/December 1990, p 12.

page 100. From Berosini interviews, October 1991-92.

page 101. From an article by George Bennett titled "PETA kills 'rescued animals,'" printed in the *Montgomery Journal* (Maryland), April 11, 1991, p A1.

page 103. From *Berousek a.k.a. Berosini vs. People for the Ethical Treatment of Animals*.

**Chapter 9**

page 124. From an article titled "Physicians and the Animal Rights Movement, " by Herbert Pardes, MD., Anne West, and Harold Alan Pincus, MD, printed in *The New England Journal of Medicine*, June 6, 1991, p 1642.

page 124. From the Spring/1992 issue of *MSU Today*.

page 125. From Sharon Schmickle's article titled "Animal-rights firebombs send meat, fur flying," printed in the *Washington Times*, November 11, 1992.

**Chapter 10**

page 129. From Ingrid Newkirk's book, *Save the Animals! 101 Easy Things You Can Do* (Warner, New York, 1990), p 1.

page 129. From *The Satanic Bible* by Anton Szandor LaVey (Avon Books, New York, 1969), p 25.

page 130. From an article by Mark LaRochelle titled "Animal 'rights' Nazis," printed in *The People's Agenda*, February 1991, p 7.

page 132. From the Roderick Frazier Nash book, p 61.

page 132. From the Nash book.

page 132. From C.G. Jung's book, *Collected Works of C.G. Jung*, Bollinger Ser., No. 20, 2nd ed. (N.J. University Press, Princeton, 1973) trans. R.F.C. Hull, Vol. 11, Psychology and Religion: West and East, p 75. This quote was more directly taken from Dr. Scott Peck's wonderful book, *The Road Less Traveled* (Simon and Schuster, 1978), p 17.

page 133. From the *Washington Post*, November 13, 1983.

page 133. From the Mark LaRochelle article.

page 134. From an article by Dr. Adrian Morrison, DVM, Ph.D., titled "My Philosophy of Animal Use in Research," printed in *Alliance Alert*, September 1992, p 3.

page 134. Quoted by permission of Robert McAfee Brown.

page 137. The seductive premise is an ends-justifies-the-means formula for selling cult principles. It offers the assurance of a perfect future world, but only if ideas of today's needs are subordinated to the means by which the cult operates.

page 137. From "American Family Foundation News," printed in *The Cult Observer*, Vol. 9 No. 9, 1992, p 18.

page 141. From the book by Coretta Scott King titled *The Words of Martin Luther King Jr.* (Newmarket, New York, 1987), p 18.

page 141. From the Patrick H. Cleveland, Ph.D. open letter to the research community titled "Animal Rights and Public Perceptions: A Dangerous Combination," undated, p 5.

# APPENDIX A

While reading this agenda summary, it must be understood that animal rights goals reach the mainstream in an assortment of various quotes, articles and books written by movement leaders, and from observations of their activities. They must be pieced together by outsiders, as they do not formally exist in a movement manifesto or party platform.

With the preceding in mind, the following section is quoted from the premier animal rights magazine, Animals' Agenda. While these points may not comprise the complete animal rights manifesto (because of the hidden, subversive nature of the overall movement), they do have an extra measure of legitimacy when compared to other available writings because these items formed the "animal liberation plank" offered by animal rightists for inclusion in the U.S. Green platform in 1987. This, then, is considered sanitized enough for public consumption. More radical positions can certainly be found deeper within the movement.

**Animal Rights Platform**
Reprinted from the Animals' Agenda, 456 Turnpike, Monroe CT 06468, November 1987, VII No. 9, pp 12-16;

1. We are firmly committed to the eventual abolition by law of animal research, and call for an immediate prohibition of painful experiments and tests. The billions of dollars disbursed annually by the National Institutes of Health for animal experiments should be rechanneled into direct health care, preventive medicine, and biomedical research using non-animal tests and procedures. In addition, the government should fund projects to develop and promote non-animal technologies where they do not yet exist so that animal experiments may be rapidly phased out. In the meantime, procedural mechanisms must be established to allow for greater public scrutiny of all research using animals.

2. The use of animals for cosmetics and household product testing, tobacco and alcohol testing, psychological testing, classroom demonstration and dissection, and in weapons development or other warfare programs must be outlawed immediately.

3. We encourage vegetarianism for ethical, ecological and health reasons. As conversion of plant protein to animal flesh for human consumption is an energetically inefficient means of food production, a vegetarian diet allows for a wiser use of the world's limited food resources. Livestock production is a major source of environmental degradation. Further, a shift in human diet from animal foods to plant food would result in a lower incidence of heart diseases and cancer and better health generally. Vegetarian meals should be made available to all public institutions including primary and secondary schools. Nutritional education programs currently administered by the Department of Agriculture should be handled by an agency charged with promoting public health rather than promoting the interest of agribusiness.

4. Steps should be taken to begin phasing out intensive confinement systems of livestock production, also called factory farming, which causes severe physical and psychological suffering for the animals kept in overcrowded and unnatural conditions. As animal agriculture depletes and pollutes water and soil resources, and destroys forests and other ecosystems, we call for the eventual elimination of animal agriculture. In the meantime, the exportation of live farm animals for overseas slaughter should be banned and domestic transportation and slaughter of animals must be regulated to ensure humane treatment. Livestock grazing on U.S. public lands should be immediately prohibited. Internationally, the United States should assist poorer countries in developing locally-based, self-reliant agricultural systems.

5. The use of herbicides, pesticides, and other toxic agricultural chemicals should be phased out. Predator control on public lands should be immediately outlawed, and steps should be taken to reintroduce native predators to areas from which they have been eradicated in order to restore the balance of nature.

6. Responsibility for enforcement of animal welfare legislation must be transferred from the Department of Agriculture to an agency created for the purpose of protecting animals and the environment.

7. Commercial trapping and fur ranching should be eliminated. We call for an end to the use of furs while recognizing Western society's responsibility to support alternative livelihood for native peoples who now rely on trapping because of the colonial European and North American fur industries.

8. Hunting, trapping, and fishing for sport should be prohibited. State and Federal wildlife agencies should focus on preserving and re-establishing habitat for wild animals, instead of practicing game species management for maximum sustainable yield. Where possible, native species, including predators, should be reintroduced to areas from which they have been eradicated. Protection of native animals and plants in their natural surroundings must be given priority over economic development plans. Further, drainage of wetlands and development of shore areas must be stopped immediately.

9. Internationally, steps should be taken by the U.S. government to prevent further destruction of rainforests. Additionally, we call on the U.S. government to act aggressively to end the international trade in wildlife and goods produced from exotic and/or endangered fauna or flora.

10. We strongly discourage any further breeding of companion animals, including pedigreed or purebred dogs and cats. Spay and neuter clinics should be subsidized by state and municipal governments. Commerce in domestic and exotic animals for the pet trade should be abolished.

11. We call for an end to the use of animals in entertainment and sports such as horse and dog racing, dog and cock fighting, fox hunting, hare coursing, rodeos, circuses and other spectacles, and a critical reappraisal of the use of animals in quasi-educational institutions such as zoos and aquariums. These institutions, guided not by humane concerns but by market imperatives, often

cruelly treat animals and act as agents of destruction for wild animals. In general, we believe that animals should be left in their appropriate environments in the wild, and not showcased for entertainment purposes. Any animals held captive must have their physiological, behavioral, and social needs satisfied.

12. Advances in biotechnology are posing a threat to the integrity of species, which may ultimately reduce all living beings to the level of patentable commodities. Genetic manipulation of species to produce transgenic animals should be prohibited.

## Reported Animal Rights Activists Groups

Action for Animals
Oakland, CA and Bend, OR

Alliance for Animals, The
Boston, MA

Alliance for Research Accountability (ARA)
Ventura, CA

American Anti-Vivisection Society
Philadelphia, PA

American Vegan Society
Mlaga, NJ

American Vegetarians
Akron, OH

Animal Advocates, Inc.
Pittsburgh, PA

Animal Aid
Portland, OR

Animal Defense Legion
Santa Rosa, CA

Animal Liberation Front
Support Group of America (ALFSGA)
San Bernardino, CA

Animal Liberation League
Arlington, TX

Animal Rights Action League (ARAL)
Saratoga Springs, NY

Animal Rights Community (ARC)
Cincinnati, OH

Animal Rights Connection
San Francisco, CA

Animal Rights Forum
Montpelier, VT

Animal Rights of Texas (ART)
Fort Worth, TX

Animal Rights Information and Education
Service (Aries)
Rowayton, CT

Animal Rights Mobilization (ARM)
(formerly Trans-Species Unlimited)
Williamsport, PA

Animal Welfare Institute (AWI)
Washington, D.C.

Animals Emancipation
Goleta, CA

Animals Lobby
Sacramento, CA

Argus Archives
New York, NY

Arizonians for Safety and Humanity
on Public Lands
Phoenix, AZ

AHIMSA
Canada

Beauty Without Cruelty
New York, NY

Berkeley Students for Animal Liberation
Berkeley, CA

Between the Species
Berkeley, CA

Bluegrass Animal Welfare League, Inc. (BAWL)
Lexington, KY

Brighton Students for Peaceful Change (BSFPC)
Rochester, NY

Californians for the Ethical Treatment of Animals (CETA)
Morongo Valley, CA

Carriage Horse Action Committee
New York, NY

Citizens' for Animals Resources and Environment (CARE)
Milwaukee, WI

Citizens to End Animal Suffering and Exploitation (CEASE)
Cambridge, MA

Coalition Against Fur Farms
Ashland, OR

Coalition for Pet Population Control
Los Angeles, CA

Coalition to Update Research and Education, The
New York, NY

Committee to Abolish Sport Hunting (CASH)
White Plains, NY

Earth First!
California


Earth Island Institute
San Francisco, CA

Earthtrust
Honolulu, HI

Elsa Wild Animal Appeal
Elmhurst, IL

End Dogs on Earth Now! (EDEN!)
United States (underground)

Environmental Investigation Agency
Washington, D.C.

Farm Sanctuary
Rockland, DE

Feminist for Animal Rights
Berkeley, CA

Florida Action for Animals (FAFA)
Stuart, FL

Friends of Animals (FOA)
Norwalk, CT

Friends of Beaversprite
Little Falls, NY

Fund for Animals (FFA)
New York, NY

Global Investigations
Scotts Valley, CA

Good Shepherd Foundation
Nevada City, CA

Greenpeace
International

Hawaii Animal Welfare Cooperative
Hilo, HI

Houston Animal Rights Team, Inc. (HART)
Houston, TX

Humane Society of Charlotte
Charlotte, NC

Hunt Saboteurs
Santa Cruz, CA

In Defense of Animals
San Rafael, CA

Independent Animal Activists' Network (IAAN)
Sioux Falls, SD

International Primate Protection League
Summerville, SC

Jehovah's Witnesses for Animal Rights
Sunnyvale, CA

Kalamazoo-Area Animal Liberation League
Kalamazoo, MI

Last Chance for Animals
Tarzana, CA

Lifeline for Animals
Stony Point, NY

Mobilization for Animals
Pittsburgh, PA

National Alliance for Animals
Washington, D.C.

National Animal Legal Foundation (NALF)
Sacramento, CA

National Anti-Vivisection Society (NAVS)
London, England

New England Anti-Vivisection Society
Boston, MA

Noah's Friends
Richmond, VA

North Carolina Network for Animals (NCNA)
Greensboro, NC

Ohio Humane Education Association
Asheville, NC

Orange County People for Animals
Santa Ana, CA

People for the Ethical Treatment of Animals (PETA)
Rockville, MD

Performing Animals Welfare Society (PAWS)
Galt, CA

Physicians Committee for Responsible Medicine (PCRM)
Washington, D.C.

Progressive Animal Welfare Society (PAWS)
Seattle, WA

Rocky Mountain Humane Society (RMHS)
Littleston, CO

Sarasota in Defense of Animals (SIDA)
Sarasota, FL

Sea Shepherd Conservation Society
Redondo Beach, CA

Society for Animal Rights
Liano, CA

Society of Activist Vegetarians (SAVE)
Charleston, WV

Students United Protesting Research Experiments on Sentient Subjects (SUPRESS)
Pasadena, CA

Tennessee Network for Animals
Knoxville and Nashville, TN

Voices for Animals
Charlottesville, VA

Western North Carolina Animal Rights Coalition
Asheville, NC

Wild Horse and Burro Sanctuary
Shingletown, CA

Woodstock Animal Rights Movement (WARM)
Woodstock, NY

Zero Population Growth
Washington, D.C.

*Vivisection is monstrous. Medical science has little to learn, and nothing can be gained by repetition of experiments on living animals.*
Sir George Duckett, head of the Society for the Abolition of Vivisection in England, 1875

## Medical Advances through Animal Research and Testing in the 20th Century

**Early 1900s**
Treatment of pellagra (Niacin deficiency) and rickets (Vitamin D deficiency)
Electrocardiography and cardiac catheterization

**1920s**
Discovery of thyroxin
Intravenous feeding
Discovery of insulin for diabetes control

**1930s**
Therapeutic use of sulfa drugs
Prevention of tetanus
Development of anticoagulants, modern anesthesia and neuromuscular blocking agents

**1940s**
Treatment of rheumatoid arthritis and whooping cough
Therapeutic use of antibiotics, such as penicillin aureomycin and streptomycin
Discovery of the Rh factor
Treatment of leprosy
Prevention of diptheria

**1950s**
Prevention of poliomyelitis
Development of cancer chemotherapy
Open-heart surgery and cardiac pacemaker

**1960s**
Prevention of rubella
Corneal transplant
Coronary bypass surgery
Therapeutic use of cortisone
Development of radioimmunoassay for measurement of minute quantities of antibodies, hormones and other substances in the body
Discovery of anti-hypertensive drugs

**1970s**
Prevention of measles
Eradication of smallpox
Modern treatment of coronary insufficiency
Heart transplant
Development of non-addictive painkillers
Discovery of oncogenes
Laser treatment to prevent blindness
Recombinant DNA technology
Improved matching of donated kidneys with recipients
First antiviral drugs
Development of monoclonal antibodies
Principles of intensive care
Beneficial effects of exercise on heart

**1980s**
Use of cyclosporin and other anti-rejection drugs for organ transplants
Artificial heart transplants
Identification of psychophysiological factors in depression, anxiety and phobia
Deprenyl for Parkinson's disease
Improved detection and therapy for breast cancer
Hepatitis B vaccine
AZT for treating AIDS
Cochlear implants for deafness
Methylprednisolone for spinal-cord injury
In vitro fertilization
Cholesterol-lowering drugs
Discovery of tumor suppressor genes
Process of metastasis
Curative drugs for childhood leukemia
Lyme disease diagnostic test

**Organizations Promoting Responsible Use of Animals**

American Animal Welfare Foundation
Marcia Kelly, Program Director
405 Sibley St  St. Paul, MN 55101
(612) 293-0349

Americans for Medical Progress, Inc.
Crystal Square Three
1735 Jefferson Davis Hwy # 907
Arlington VA 22202
703) 486-1411; FAX (703) 486-1416

Coalition for Animals & Animal Research (CFAAR)
PO Box 8060
Berkeley CA 94707-8060

Coalition for Animals & Animal Research (CFAAR)
PO Box 22441
San Diego CA 92192

Foundation for Biomedical Research
Mary Brennan, vice president
818 Connecticut Ave NW #303
Washington D.C. 20006
(202) 457-0654

Incurably Ill for Animal Research (IIFAR)
PO Box 27454
Lansing MI 48909
(517) 887-1141

National Animal Interest Alliance
Patti Strand, Executive Director
PO Box 66579, Portland OR 97290
(503) 761-8962 (phone/fax)

Putting People First
4401 Connecticut Ave NW # 310-A
Washington, D.C. 20008
(202) 364-7277

The American Society for the
Prevention of Cruelty
to Animals

441 East 92nd Street
New York, New York 10128

Please make your check payable to the ASPCA
and mail it with this survey in the enclosed postage-
paid envelope. Your contribution is tax-deductible
to the extent allowed by law.

Please note that you may be able to *double* your
support—at no cost to yourself—if your employer
sponsors a matching gift program. Check with
your personnel or contributions office for further
details.

☐ Please send me information on how to make
H    a bequest.

☐ **YES**, I want to help the ASPCA put an end to the suffering once and for all.
I enclose my membership contribution of:

☐ $20 Regular Member    ☐ $500 Founder's Society Friend
☐ $50 Supporting Member    ☐ $1,000 Founder's Society Associate
☐ $100 Sustaining Member    ☐ $____Other

☐ I have filled out my 1991 ANIMAL PROTECTION SURVEY below.
*With $20 or more you'll receive your FREE copy of The Animal Rights Handbook

II.I.I..I.I.I.I.I.III.I.I..I.I.II..I.IIII.I

---

SURVEY NO: 98F231R

# 1991
## ASPCA ANIMAL PROTECTION
### ★ SURVEY ★

★ DEADLINE DATE: 10 DAYS AFTER RECEIPT ★

INSTRUCTIONS: Please read the enclosed
letter before answering the survey questions.
After completing the survey, return this entire
form in the enclosed postage-paid envelope.
Estimated time of completion: 6 minutes.

FOR INTERNAL USE ONLY
DATE SURVEY REC'D:    __/__/__
DATE SURVEY TABULATED:    __/__/__
TABULATOR'S INITIALS:_____

1) LAB TESTING: In a leading biomedical research
laboratory, an undercover investigator recently
discovered such horrifying practices as experimenting on live puppies, deliberately drowning cats with
salt water, and dissecting animals while they were
still alive. Nevertheless, many scientists continue to
protest that the use of animals in medical research
has led to important medical breakthroughs over the
years—especially in the areas of transplants and
artificial organs and in developing vaccines. Where
do you stand on the ethics of using animals for
laboratory testing?

☐ a. All use of animals in lab tests is wrong.

☐ b. Laboratory testing is permissible only if it is
likely to yield valuable new information on
life threatening diseases.

☐ c. Laboratory testing is permissible only if it is
likely to yield valuable information *and* every
precaution is taken not to cause the animal
pain.

☐ d. All lab tests are permissible, including those
testing the lethal or caustic nature of cosmetics
and detergents.

2) BREAK-INS AND SEIZURE: Laboratories experimenting on animals have been broken into, records
confiscated, and animals removed, in an effort to
call attention to poor living conditions and experiments that cause animal pain and suffering. Individuals wearing fur coats have been angrily confronted
on the street, and in some instances stores selling
furs have been vandalized. Where do you stand on
the issue of using such tactics to protect the right
animals have not to be abused?

☐ a. Violence is always wrong.

☐ b. Violence is not desirable, but it is permissible
to damage property to save an animal's life.

☐ c. Protecting animals from human cruelty requires whatever means are necessary.

Printed on recycled paper ♻    continued ♦

---

# 1991
# ASPCA ANIMAL PROTECTION
# ★ SURVEY ★

3) **FUR TRAPPING AND FUR RANCHING:** The slaughter of trapped and ranch-raised animals solely for the manufacture of fur garments is a major concern of the animal protection movement. The fur manufacturers counter with charges of hypocrisy on the part of those who protest but still eat meat and use leather products. Where do you stand on this issue?

☐ a. It is worse to trap or raise animals solely for their fur than it is to raise animals for meat and leather products.

☐ b. A truly humane society should avoid meat, leather, and fur.

☐ c. Raising animals for their fur is no worse than raising animals for meat and leather.

☐ d. Humane progress is slow and the anti-fur campaign is an appropriate focus now.

4) **FACTORY FARMING:** Nowhere in the field of animal protection is there more controversy today than when it comes to raising billions of animals for food each year. What's your opinion?

☐ a. All animals may be used for human food.

☐ b. All use of animals for food is morally wrong.

☐ c. Only animals raised humanely should be used for food.

☐ d. Only the by-products of animals should be used for food, i.e., milk and eggs.

5) **ENTERTAINMENT:** The use of animals in entertainment is a complicated issue. While most people would strongly object to cockfighting and dogfighting, for example, the use of animals in such entertainments as motion pictures, rodeos, circuses, horse races, dog races, aquariums, and zoos is more controversial. Where do you stand on the ethics of using animals for the amusement of humans?

☐ a. All use of animals for human entertainment is morally wrong.

☐ b. Animals may be used for entertainment as long as they are treated humanely.

☐ c. Only "blood sports" like cockfighting are ethically wrong.

6) **HUNTING, FISHING AND WILD ANIMALS:** The founder of the ASPCA, Henry Bergh, popularized the clay pigeon as an alternative to the cruel practice of target shooting on live birds. Many hunters are avid conservationists and responsible pet owners. Yet many animal protection activists think all hunting is wrong. What's your opinion?

☐ a. All forms of hunting and fishing are morally permissible.

☐ b. Hunting baited or captive animals is always wrong, but hunting wild animals is morally permissible as long as the hunter eats whatever he kills.

☐ c. Hunting is justifiable if the species in question is overpopulated and needs to be culled, but it is morally wrong if the species is threatened or endangered.

☐ d. Hunting is morally wrong, but fishing is not.

☐ e. All hunting and fishing is wrong.

7) **PRIORITIES:** Which of these do you *personally* consider the single most pressing issue in the field of animal protection? (Check only one)

☐ a. Wild animals    ☐ f. Animals in entertainment
☐ b. Laboratory animals    ☐ g. Food animals
☐ c. Animals raised for fur    ☐ h. Hunting and fishing
☐ d. Pet overpopulation    ☐ i. Working animals
☐ e. Cult sacrifice    ☐ j. Animal fighting

8) **Would you be willing to contribute to help the ASPCA's historic efforts to prevent cruelty to all animals everywhere?**

☐ Yes    ☐ No

If your answer is "yes," please fill out the form above the questionnaire and mail this entire document along with your check (made payable to the ASPCA) in the enclosed postage-paid envelope today.

Your compassionate support of our efforts to help all creatures is much appreciated. Thank you!

A financial report and specific information on ASPCA programs, activities and grants to non-affiliated organizations are available on request from the ASPCA. A financial report is also available from the New York State Department of State, Office of Charities Registration, Albany, New York 12231.

## ANIMAL RIGHTS — A QUESTION OF CONSCIENCE

*PLEASE RESPOND WITHIN 10 DAYS!*

Prepared for:

**INSTRUCTIONS: Please indicate your answers with a check mark in the appropriate box. Then return your form in the enclosed postage-paid envelope.** <u>Note</u>: Your name, address and responses will remain completely confidential when referendum results are tabulated.

1. Before reading this mailing, were you aware of the vast numbers of animals who suffer and perish every year in American research laboratories? ☐ Yes ☐ No

2. Did you realize that the vast majority of painful animal experimentation has no relation at all to human survival or the elimination of disease? ☐ Yes ☐ No

3. Do you approve of lethal animal experimentation to test new cosmetics and household products? ☐ Yes ☐ No

4. Do you approve of military testing of new weapons, poison gases and radiation on live animals? ☐ Yes ☐ No

5. Would you support Congressional legislation such as the Consumer Products Safe Testing Act extending protection to all experimental subjects? (Nearly 90% are currently excluded from any protection.) ☐ Yes ☐ No

6. Would you like to see your tax dollars directed toward research that emphasizes alternatives to animal experimentation? ☐ Yes ☐ No

7. Do you see any need for a major public education effort to expand awareness about animal rights? ☐ Yes ☐ No

8. Would you consider altering your consumer habits, and even some of the foods you eat, in order to reduce animal suffering—particularly if there were health benefits?
☐ Absolutely ☐ Probably ☐ Possibly ☐ Unlikely

9. Do you feel that peaceful yet illegal activities are ever justified when their aim is the rescue of suffering animals?
☐ Usually ☐ Sometimes ☐ Not often ☐ Never

over ♻ Recycled Paper

— 168 —

# DORIS DAY
# ANIMAL LEAGUE

Enclosed is your 1992 National
Animal Protection Opinion Poll
Please verify your poll number.

Dear Friend:

Do you have strong opinions about the cruel mistreatment of helpless animals?

Are you outraged when you hear of animals being tortured and killed in useless "experiments" which serve no valid medical or scientific purpose?

If you are like me, you do have strong views about a number of important issues which affect the lives, health and safety of our animal friends.

And, if you are like me, you want your Representatives in Washington to know your opinions so they will take action on animal protection issues in 1992.

I have enclosed a copy of our National Animal Protection Opinion Poll for 1992 which I hope that you will fill out and return today. The results will be delivered to your elected Representatives.

**Issue #1 in your Animal Protection Poll involves the notorious LD-50 Test.** In this barbaric experiment researchers attempt to discover how much of a product will kill 50% of the animals in a test group.

Defenseless animals are force fed floor wax, oven cleaner, bleach and other dangerous substances - often with horrible results.

Not only is this test cruel, it is useless and outdated as well. Prominent scientists agree that there are far better ways to test the safety of products than by pouring them down the throats of helpless animals.

The LD-50 Test is no longer required by the Food and Drug Administration. Even the American Pharmaceutical Association admits it "lacks justification."

(please turn page)

Issue #2 in your Animal Protection Poll is the Draize Rabbit Eye Test in which these rabbits are locked into stocks with their heads sticking out, while "researchers" go down the line, injecting anything from cosmetics to pesticides into their eyes!

The pain is so terrible some of them break their backs trying to wriggle out of the stocks.

This barbaric test is supposed to tell if these products are safe for human use. The problem is that rabbits' eyes are totally different from human eyes and those tests don't give accurate data.

The Doris Day Animal League is working with concerned Members of Congress to outlaw the Draize Test and the LD-50 Test. Your Animal Protection Poll will let your elected Representatives know if you support our efforts.

Issue #3 in your Animal Protection Poll is "pound seizure" - the practice of selling pound animals to research laboratories. Many of these animals were household pets, like your dog and cat. Some were abandoned. Others simply got lost. The Doris Day Animal League believes that pounds should care for these animals and work for their adoption into loving families -- not sell them to laboratories where they will be tortured or killed.

Issue #4 in your Animal Protection Poll covers other kinds of animal sellers, the so-called "puppy mills." These are commercial dog breeding factories which sell puppies to pet stores throughout the United States. Humane workers have found many of these facilities to be virtual concentration camps -- overcrowded cages filled with filthy, starving, diseased animals. The Doris Day Animal League has been lobbying the Department of Agriculture to enforce laws which would require severe penalties for puppy mill operators who neglect or abuse their animals.

Issue #5 in your Animal Protection Poll discusses another commercial use of animals which has recently generated headlines -- the sale of fur coats. The invention of synthetic fabrics has done away with the argument that people "need" fur to protect them against cold weather. The killing of animals for their pelts is cruel and unnecessary. Your poll asks you whether we should stop the sale of fur coats nationally.

Issue #6 is perhaps the most controversial of all. It deals with ritual animal sacrifices which are regularly performed by "religious cults." Believe it or not, these cultists argue that their activities should be protected by "freedom of religion." I

(next page please)

# NATIONAL ANIMAL PROTECTION OPINION POLL

COMMISSIONED BY:
Doris Day, President
Doris Day Animal League
900 2nd Street, N.E., Suite 303
Washington, D.C. 20002
X291

## INSTRUCTIONS — IMPORTANT — PLEASE READ

Please complete questions and return the poll in the enclosed reply envelope within 24 hours. For further information about the issues presented in this poll, consult your letter from Doris Day.

### ISSUE #1 LD-50 Test

Should Congress outlaw experiments which require animals to be poisoned in order to test household products?

☐ Yes          ☐ No

### ISSUE #2 Draize Rabbit Eye Test

Should Congress outlaw tests which require cosmetics, pesticides and other toxic substances to be injected into the eyes of rabbits?

☐ Yes          ☐ No

### ISSUE #3 Pound Seizure

Should Congress prohibit pounds from selling dogs, cats and other animals to research laboratories and commercial testing facilities?

☐ Yes          ☐ No

### ISSUE #4 "Puppy Mills"

Should the Department of Agriculture enforce regulations which require strict penalties for commercial animal sellers who neglect or abuse animals?

☐ Yes          ☐ No

### ISSUE #5 Fur Coats

Should Congress ban the sale of fur coats in the United States?

☐ Yes          ☐ No

### ISSUE #6 Animal Sacrifice

Should Congress make it illegal for "religious cults" to mutilate, torture or kill animals?

☐ Yes          ☐ No

### ISSUE #7 What Will You Do To Protect Animals?

Will you join the Doris Day Animal League and help us end the cruel abuse of innocent animals?

☐ Yes          ☐ No

Please indicate the amount you will contribute to help us defeat the powerful cosmetic companies, consumer products manufacturers and other uncaring special interests who oppose us in this fight.

☐ $25          ☐ $15          ☐ $10

☐ $50          ☐ Other $ _____

For $10 or more you will receive a Membership Card, "Stop Animal Abuse" bumper sticker and autographed picture. Also a subscription to "Animal Guardian."

• • •

Contributions or gifts to DDAL are not tax-deductible. This is because the law does not permit a deduction for contributions to any organization primarily engaged in lobbying for legislation.

*Thank you for your help.*

# BIBLIOGRAPHY

Anderson, William. *Green Man*, London: Harper Collins, 1990.

Budiansky, Stephen. *The Covenant of the Wild*, New York: William Morrow, 1992.

Campbell, Joseph. *The Mythic Image*, Princeton: Princeton University Press, 1974.

Carson, Gerald. *Men, Beasts and Gods*, New York: Charles Scribner's Sons, 1972.

Carter, Carolle. *The Shamrock and the Swastika*, Palo Alto: Pacific Books, 1977.

Cesaresco, Countess Evelyn Martinengo. *The Place of Animals in Human Thought*, New York: Charles Scribner's Sons, 1909.

Conway, Flo and Jim Siegelman. *Holy Terror*, New York: Doubleday, 1982.

Cooper, John Charles. *The New Mentality*, Philadelphia: Westminster Press, 1969.

Corson, John J. *Business in the Humane Society*, New York: McGraw Hill, 1971.

Ed. Morris, Richard Knowles and Michael W. Fox. *On the Fifth Day*, Contributors: Robert S. Brumbaugh, et al. Washington, D. C.: Acropolis, 1978.

Ed. GIllespie, Angus K. and Jay Mechling. *American Wildlife in Symbol and Story*, Knoxville, University of Tennessee, 1987.

Ed. Lochner, Louis P. *The Goebbels Diaries 1942-1943*, New York: Doubleday, 1948.

Ed. Larrabee, Harold A. *Bentham's Handbook of Political Fallacies*, Baltimore, Johns Hopkins, 1952.

Fox, Dr. Michael W. *Inhumane Society,* New York: St. Martins, 1990.

Hardy, David T.,Esq. *America's New Extremists,* Washington, D.C.: Washington Legal Foundation, 1990.

Henshaw, David. *Animal Warfare,* London: Fontana, 1989.

Hobbes, Thomas. *Leviathan,* London: J. M. Dent & Sons, 1965.

Hoffer, Eric. *The True Believer,* New York: Harper & Rowe, 1951.

Hunt, Morton. *The Compassionate Beast,* New York: William Morrow, 1990.

Jasper, James M., and Dorothy Nelkin. *The Animal Rights Crusade,* New York, 1992.

Kuhse, Helga and Peter Singer. *Should the Baby Live?,* Oxford: Oxford University Press, 1985.

Manes, Christopher. *Green Rage,* Boston: Little, Brown, 1990.

Mill, John Stuart. *Principles of Political Economy, Vol. I & II,* New York: Appleton, 1889.

Nash, Roderick Frazier. *The Rights of Nature,* Madison: University of Wisconsin Press, 1989.

Newkirk, Ingrid. *Save the Animals,* New York: Warner, 1990.

Nietzsche, Frederich. *The Philosophy of Nietzsche,* New York: The Modern Library, 1954.

Ogden, C. K. *Bentham's Theory of Fictions,* New York: Harcourt, Brace, 1932.

Parker, James. *Man and Beast He Preserves, Humans and Animals in the Bible and Jewish and Christian Traditions,* Portland: Parker, 1991.

Paine, Thomas. *Rights of Man,* New York: Prometheus, 1987.

Ray, Dixie Lee and Lou Guzzo. *Trashing the Planet,* Washington, D. C. Regnery Gateway, 1990.

Regan, Tom. *The Thee Generation,* Philadelphia: Temple University Press, 1991.

Regan, Tom. *The Case for Animal Rights,* Berkeley and Los Angeles: University of California Press, 1983.

Roberts, Richard. *Tales for Jung Folk*, San Anselmo: Vernal Equinox Press, 1983.

Rollin, Bernard. *Animal Rights and Human Morality*, New York: Prometheus, 1981.

Sapontzis, S. F. Morals, *Reason and Animals*, Philadelphia: Temple University Press, 1987.

Singer, Peter. *Animal Liberation*, New York: Random House, 1975.

Spiegal, Marjorie. *The Dreaded Comparison*, Philadelphia: New Society, 1988.

Stewart, Hillary. *Totem Poles*, Seattle: University of Washington Press, 1990.

Stone, Christopher D. *Should Trees Have Standing?*, Los Altos: William Kaufman, 1974.

Thoreau, Henry David. *Anti-Slavery and Reform Papers*, Montreal: Harvest House, 1963.

Tobias, Michael, et al. *Deep Ecology*, San Marcos: Avant, 1988.

Toland, John. *Adolph Hitler, vol. I & II*, New York: Doubleday, 1976.

Turner, E. S. *All Heaven in a Rage*, New York: St. Martin's, 1965.

Welsh, Heidi J. *Animal Testing and Consumer Products*, Washington, D.C.: Investor Responsibility Research Center, 1990.

Wollstonecraft, Mary. *A Vindication of the Rights of Woman*, Ed. Carol H. Poston. New York: W. W. Norton, 1975.

**PERIODICALS**

Ed. Bartlett, Kim. *The Animals' Agenda*, Monroe, CT: Animal Rights Network.

Ed. Rowan, Andrew. *Anthrozoos*, Boston: University Press of New England, Hanover and London.

■ In Ireland, members of the Animal Liberation Front told the news media that they had laced bottles of shampoo with bleach in three cities to protest the manufacturer's use of animals for cosmetic research. Bottles of the shampoo were removed from shelves in Dublin, Limerick and Kilkenny. (1985)

■ In Great Britain, 13 animal rights activists were tried and found guilty for what had been described as one of the most violent and well-organized assaults on a research institution in Europe. The convicted individuals had participated in an April 1985 raid on the Imperial Chemical Industries' Alderly Park site. The raid was conducted by 300 masked Animal Liberation Front members who, armed with crowbars, smashed windows and doors to break into several buildings. Animals and reports were stolen and more than $15,000 in damages were done to the facilities. (June 7, 1985)

■ The Animal Liberation Front vandalized 11 Jaguar automobiles owned by a car-rental company in Thames Ditton, Surrey, England. The motive for the attack, according to investigators, was ALF's discovery that the company had been renting cars to police officers for following animal activists in London. (1985)

■ The Animal Liberation Front claimed responsibility for a break-in at the University of Toronto's dentistry building which caused more than $7,000 in damages, according to the Chronicle of Higher Education. ALF stated in a press release that the break-in was part of its "economic sabotage campaign against the scums who torture animals." Unable to get into the building's animal research facility, which they called, "an animal concentration camp," members of the group spray-painted corridors and laboratories and destroyed equipment. (February 1986)

■ Seven firebombs were left at a South London department store that sells fur coats, according to the Daily Express, a British newspaper. The Animal Liberation Front was responsible for the firebombs, according to the newspaper which cited information obtained by its own reporter during a three-month undercover assignment. The first-person account described meetings during which ALF members revealed plans to kidnap a member of the royal family, bomb the homes of scientists and doctors, burn research facilities to the ground, and terrorize the homes of certain police officers. In a front-page editorial accompanying the story, the newspaper called the activities of ALF "so close to terrorism...as to be indistinguishable from it." The newspaper reported that Scotland Yard tracks ALF's activities daily, aided by computer information on more than 1,000 sympathizers. (May 5, 1986)

■ Using videotapes and photographs, animal rights activists have portrayed the eye injuries of a laboratory animal as evidence of abusive handling by scientists at the University of California, Riverside. A story, "Activists likely caused injuries to animals 'freed' from lab, report says," published by The Atlanta Constitution, quoted a National Institutes of Health Office for Protection from Research Risks report that the injuries must have occurred after the monkey was stolen from the university by the Animal Liberation Front. The newspaper story stated that "heavy bandages kept over the monkey's eyes apparently were removed by activists after the raid and replaced with thinner ones that didn't prevent the animal from scratching the sutures holding his eyelids shut. The eye [injuries] in the monkey, NIH said, probably were caused by the animal's post-raid scratching." (July 3, 1986)

■ California Attorney General John Van de Kamp submitted to the state Legislature a report on organized crime in California that identified the Animal Liberation Front as an active "terrorist group" in the state. (July 23, 1986)

■ A veterinary diagnostic center under construction at the University of California, Davis was destroyed by a fire that police believe was ignited by the Animal Liberation Front. The fire gutted the $10 million research facility that was intended to provide animal diagnostic services and disease surveillance. In addition to the fire, 18 university vehicles were vandalized. The letters "ALF" were painted on a wall. Lavonne Bishop of the Animal Rights Direct Action Coalition stated: "We don't condone violence, but we applaud the ALF...I'm glad they did it. I hope they do more of it." (April 16, 1987)